Excel 2010: Intermediate

Student Manual

Excel 2010: Intermediate

President, Axzo Press:	Jon Winder
Vice President, Product Development:	Charles G. Blum
Vice President, Operations:	Josh Pincus
Director of Publishing Systems Development:	Dan Quackenbush
Developmental Editor:	Laurie Perry
Copyeditor:	Catherine Oliver
Keytester:	Cliff Coryea

Trademarks

ILT Series is a trademark of Axzo Press.

Some of the product names and company names used in this book have been used for identification purposes only and may be trademarks or registered trademarks of their respective manufacturers and sellers.

Disclaimer

We reserve the right to revise this publication and make changes from time to time in its content without notice.

Student Manual
ISBN 13: 978-1-4260-2946-2

Printed in the United States of America

3 4 5 6 7 8 9 10 GL 15 14 13 12

What is the Microsoft ® Office Specialist Program?

The Microsoft Office Specialist Program enables candidates to show that they have something exceptional to offer – proven expertise in certain Microsoft programs. Recognized by businesses and schools around the world, over 4 million certifications have been obtained in over 100 different countries. The Microsoft Office Specialist Program is the only Microsoft-approved certification program of its kind.

What is the Microsoft Office Specialist Certification?

The Microsoft Office Specialist certification validates through the use of exams that you have obtained specific skill sets within the applicable Microsoft Office programs and other Microsoft programs included in the Microsoft Office Specialist Program. The candidate can choose which exam(s) they want to take according to which skills they want to validate.

The available Microsoft Office Specialist Program exams include*:

- Using Windows Vista®
- Using Microsoft® Office Word 2007
- Using Microsoft® Office Word 2007 - Expert
- Using Microsoft® Office Excel® 2007
- Using Microsoft® Office Excel® 2007 - Expert
- Using Microsoft® Office PowerPoint® 2007
- Using Microsoft® Office Access® 2007
- Using Microsoft® Office Outlook® 2007
- Using Microsoft SharePoint® 2007

The Microsoft Office Specialist Program 2010 exams will include*:

- Microsoft Word 2010
- Microsoft Word 2010 Expert
- Microsoft Excel® 2010
- Microsoft Excel® 2010 Expert
- Microsoft PowerPoint® 2010
- Microsoft Access® 2010
- Microsoft Outlook® 2010
- Microsoft SharePoint® 2010

What does the Microsoft Office Specialist Approved Courseware logo represent?

The logo indicates that this courseware has been approved by Microsoft to cover the course objectives that will be included in the relevant exam. It also means that after utilizing this courseware, you may be better prepared to pass the exams required to become a certified Microsoft Office Specialist.

For more information:

To learn more about Microsoft Office Specialist exams, visit www.microsoft.com/learning/msbc

To learn about other Microsoft approved courseware from Axzo Press, visit http://www.axzopress.com.

Downloads → ILT → EXCEL 2010 INTERMEDIATE
↳ DESKTOP APPS
MS OFFICE
OFFICE 2010
EXCEL 2010
EXCEL 2010 INTERMEDIATE
— DOWNLOAD —
> STUDENT DATA
> SOLUTIONS

Contents

Introduction

After reading this introduction, you will know how to:

A Use ILT Series manuals in general.

B Use prerequisites, a target student description, course objectives, and a skills inventory to properly set your expectations for the course.

C Re-key this course after class.

Topic A: About the manual

ILT Series philosophy

Our manuals facilitate your learning by providing structured interaction with the software itself. While we provide text to explain difficult concepts, the hands-on activities are the focus of our courses. By paying close attention as your instructor leads you through these activities, you will learn the skills and concepts effectively.

We believe strongly in the instructor-led class. During class, focus on your instructor. Our manuals are designed and written to facilitate your interaction with your instructor, and not to call attention to manuals themselves.

We believe in the basic approach of setting expectations, delivering instruction, and providing summary and review afterwards. For this reason, lessons begin with objectives and end with summaries. We also provide overall course objectives and a course summary to provide both an introduction to and closure on the entire course.

Manual components

The manuals contain these major components:

- Table of contents
- Introduction
- Units
- Course summary
- Glossary
- Index

Each element is described below.

Table of contents

The table of contents acts as a learning roadmap.

Introduction

The introduction contains information about our training philosophy and our manual components, features, and conventions. It contains target student, prerequisite, objective, and setup information for the specific course.

Units

Units are the largest structural component of the course content. A unit begins with a title page that lists objectives for each major subdivision, or topic, within the unit. Within each topic, conceptual and explanatory information alternates with hands-on activities. Units conclude with a summary comprising one paragraph for each topic, and an independent practice activity that gives you an opportunity to practice the skills you've learned.

The conceptual information takes the form of text paragraphs, exhibits, lists, and tables. The activities are structured in two columns, one telling you what to do, the other providing explanations, descriptions, and graphics.

Course summary

This section provides a text summary of the entire course. It is useful for providing closure at the end of the course. The course summary also indicates the next course in this series, if there is one, and lists additional resources you might find useful as you continue to learn about the software.

Glossary

The glossary provides definitions for all of the key terms used in this course.

Index

The index at the end of this manual makes it easy for you to find information about a particular software component, feature, or concept.

Manual conventions

We've tried to keep the number of elements and the types of formatting to a minimum in the manuals. This aids in clarity and makes the manuals more classically elegant looking. But there are some conventions and icons you should know about.

Item	Description
Italic text	In conceptual text, indicates a new term or feature.
Bold text	In unit summaries, indicates a key term or concept. In an independent practice activity, indicates an explicit item that you select, choose, or type.
`Code font`	Indicates code or syntax.
`Longer strings of ▶ code will look ▶ like this.`	In the hands-on activities, any code that's too long to fit on a single line is divided into segments by one or more continuation characters (▶). This code should be entered as a continuous string of text.
Select **bold item**	In the left column of hands-on activities, bold sans-serif text indicates an explicit item that you select, choose, or type.
Keycaps like ↵ ENTER	Indicate a key on the keyboard you must press.

Hands-on activities

The hands-on activities are the most important parts of our manuals. They are divided into two primary columns. The "Here's how" column gives short instructions to you about what to do. The "Here's why" column provides explanations, graphics, and clarifications. Here's a sample:

Do it!

A-1:   Creating a commission formula

Here's how	Here's why
1 Open Sales	This is an oversimplified sales compensation worksheet. It shows sales totals, commissions, and incentives for five sales reps.
2 Observe the contents of cell F4	F4 ▼ = =E4*C_Rate The commission rate formulas use the name "C_Rate" instead of a value for the commission rate.

For these activities, we have provided a collection of data files designed to help you learn each skill in a real-world business context. As you work through the activities, you will modify and update these files. Of course, you might make a mistake and therefore want to re-key the activity starting from scratch. To make it easy to start over, you will rename each data file at the end of the first activity in which the file is modified. Our convention for renaming files is to add the word "My" to the beginning of the file name. In the above activity, for example, a file called "Sales" is being used for the first time. At the end of this activity, you would save the file as "My sales," thus leaving the "Sales" file unchanged. If you make a mistake, you can start over using the original "Sales" file.

In some activities, however, it might not be practical to rename the data file. If you want to retry one of these activities, ask your instructor for a fresh copy of the original data file.

Topic B: Setting your expectations

Properly setting your expectations is essential to your success. This topic will help you do that by providing:

- Prerequisites for this course
- A description of the target student
- A list of the objectives for the course
- A skills assessment for the course

Course prerequisites

Before taking this course, you should be familiar with personal computers and the use of a keyboard and a mouse. Furthermore, this course assumes that you've completed the following courses or have equivalent experience:

- *Windows 7: Basic*, *Windows Vista: Basic*, or *Windows XP: Basic*
- *Excel 2010: Basic*

Target student

Before taking this course, you should be comfortable using a personal computer and Microsoft Windows (preferably Windows 7). You should have some experience using Microsoft Excel. You will get the most out of this course if your goal is to become proficient in such tasks as consolidating data, using advanced chart formatting options, sorting and filtering data, using special formatting options, using templates, using error tracing features, protecting worksheets, and linking worksheets and workbooks.

Course objectives

These overall course objectives will give you an idea about what to expect from the course. It is also possible that they will help you see that this course is not the right one for you. If you think you either lack the prerequisite knowledge or already know most of the subject matter to be covered, you should let your instructor know that you think you are misplaced in the class.

Note: In addition to the general objectives listed below, specific Microsoft Office Specialist exam objectives are listed at the beginning of each topic (where applicable).

After completing this course, you will know how to:

- Link worksheets by using 3-D formulas; add a Watch window; create and manage links between workbooks; and create a workspace.

- Apply special and custom number formats; control the display of zero values; use functions to format text; create, apply, and modify styles; apply and modify themes; merge and split cells; change the orientation of data in cells; transpose data; use Paste Special operations, and add a background color and a watermark.

- Create an outline and consolidate data; create subtotals in a list; use multiple subtotal functions; and create custom views to save different sets of worksheet display and print settings.

- Define and apply cell and range names; use names in formulas; and define and apply 3-D names.

- Sort data by columns; filter data based on complex criteria and copy filtered results to another range; create, format, and name a table, and add rows and columns; and use structured references.

- Save and publish a worksheet as a Web page; insert and edit hyperlinks; publish a worksheet; and send a worksheet as an e-mail attachment.

- Format data points in charts; create combination charts and trendlines; insert sparklines; use chart templates; and add and modify drawing objects, shapes, and images.

- Use auditing features; add comments to cells and workbooks; protect a worksheet or part of a worksheet; protect the workbook structure; share, merge, and track changes in a workbook; find and remove hidden and personal data in a workbook; and mark a workbook as final.

- Change Excel's default application settings and customize the Ribbon; work with Excel templates; and create and manage templates.

- Create a PivotTable for analyzing and comparing large amounts of data; modify the PivotTable view by using slicers to filter data and by rearranging fields; improve the appearance of a PivotTable by changing its field settings and applying a style; and create a PivotChart to graphically display data from a PivotTable.

Skills inventory

Use the following form to gauge your skill level entering the class. For each skill listed, rate your familiarity from 1 to 5, with five being the most familiar. *This is not a test.* Rather, it is intended to provide you with an idea of where you're starting from at the beginning of class. If you're wholly unfamiliar with all the skills, you might not be ready for the class. If you think you already understand all of the skills, you might need to move on to the next course in the series. In either case, you should let your instructor know as soon as possible.

Skill	1	2	3	4	5
Switching between workbooks					
Copying worksheets between workbooks					
Creating 3-D formulas to link worksheets and workbooks					
Adding a Watch window					
Linking workbooks, creating external links, and redirecting links					
Creating a workspace					
Applying built-in and custom number formats					
Using functions to format text					
Creating, modifying, and applying styles					
Applying and modifying themes					
Merging and splitting cells, and changing cell orientation					
Transposing data					
Using Paste Special operations					
Adding backgrounds and watermarks					
Creating outlines to summarize and consolidate data					
Creating subtotals and using multiple subtotal functions					
Creating custom views					
Naming cells and ranges, and using names in formulas					
Modifying and deleting names					
Defining and applying 3-D names					
Sorting and filtering data					
Using advanced filtering options					

Skill	1	2	3	4	5
Creating, formatting, and modifying tables					
Using structured references in table formulas					
Calculating sum, average, and count values in a filtered table list					
Saving and publishing a worksheet as a Web page					
Inserting, editing, and deleting hyperlinks					
Sending worksheets via e-mail					
Adjusting the scale of a chart					
Creating combination charts and trendlines					
Inserting sparklines					
Using chart templates					
Inserting and formatting shapes and pictures in charts					
Using auditing features					
Adding comments to worksheets and workbooks					
Protecting a worksheet					
Protecting the workbook structure					
Sharing, merging, and tracking changes in workbooks					
Using the Document Inspector and marking workbooks as final					
Changing default application settings					
Customizing the Ribbon					
Downloading templates					
Creating and managing templates					
Creating, rearranging, and formatting PivotTables					
Using slicers to filter PivotTable data					
Creating PivotCharts					

Topic C: Re-keying the course

If you have the proper hardware and software, you can re-key this course after class. This section explains what you'll need in order to do so, and how to do it.

Hardware requirements

Your personal computer should have:

- 1 GHz or faster 32- or 64-bit processor
- At least 1 GB of RAM
- 2 GB of hard-disk space after operating system install
- Video adapter card compatible with DirectX 9 or newer, with at least 64 MB video memory
- A keyboard and a mouse
- SVGA monitor at 1024×768 resolution or higher
- Printer (useful but not required)
- DVD drive if you'll be installing via disc

Software requirements

You will also need the following software:

- Windows 7 (You can also use Windows XP or Windows Vista, but the screen shots in this course were taken in Windows 7, so your screens might look somewhat different.)
- Microsoft Office 2010
- A printer driver (An actual printer is not required, but you will not be able to get an exact preview in Print Preview without a printer driver installed.)

Network requirements

The following network components and connectivity are also required for re-keying this course:

- Internet access, for the following purposes:
    - Updating the Windows operating system and Microsoft Office 2010
    - Completing Activity B-4 in the unit titled "Advanced charting."
    - Completing Activity B-1 in the unit titled "Templates and settings."
    - Downloading the Student Data files from www.axzopress.com (if necessary)

Setup instructions to re-key the course

Before you re-key the course, you will need to perform the following steps.

1 Use Windows Update to install all available critical updates and service packs.

2 With a flat-panel display, we recommend using the panel's native resolution for best results. Color depth/quality should be set to High (24 bit) or higher.

Please note that your display settings or resolution may differ from the author's, so your screens might not exactly match the screen shots in this manual.

3   If necessary, reset any Excel 2010 defaults that you have changed. If you do not wish to reset the defaults, you can still re-key the course, but some activities might not work exactly as documented.

   a   In the Excel Options dialog box, make the following changes:

      –   On the General page, replace your name with a generic name.

      –   On the Save page, return Save Workbooks to the default file location of C:\Documents and Settings*User*\Documents.

      –   On the Advanced page, delete the custom list, show comment indicators only, and show zero values in cells.

      –   Reset the Quick Access toolbar and Ribbon to their default settings.

   b   Delete My colors and My theme. (Right-click the respective buttons on the Page Layout tab.)

   c   Delete the custom templates created in the course.

4   If you have the data disc that came with this manual, locate the Student Data folder on it and copy it to your Windows desktop.

   If you don't have the data disc, you can download the Student Data files for the course:

   a   Connect to www.axzopress.com.

   b   Under Downloads, click Instructor-Led Training.

   c   Browse the subject categories to locate your course. Then click the course title to display a list of available downloads. (You can also access these downloads through our Catalog listings.)

   d   Click the link(s) for downloading the Student Data files.

   e   On your Windows desktop, create a folder named Student Data.

   f   Double-click the downloaded zip file(s) and drag the contents into the Student Data folder.

CertBlaster software

CertBlaster pre- and post-assessment software is available for this course. To download and install this free software, complete the following steps:

1   Go to www.axzopress.com.

2   Under Downloads, click CertBlaster.

3   Click the link for Excel 2010.

4   Save the .EXE file to a folder on your hard drive. (**Note:** If you skip this step, the CertBlaster software will not install correctly.)

5   Click Start and choose Run.

6   Click Browse and navigate to the folder that contains the .EXE file.

7   Select the .EXE file and click Open.

8   Click OK and follow the on-screen instructions. When prompted for the password, enter **c_xl2010**.

Unit 1

Using multiple worksheets and workbooks

Unit time: 60 minutes

Complete this unit, and you'll know how to:

A Switch between workbooks, and copy a sheet from one workbook to another

B Create 3-D formulas to link worksheets, and add a Watch window.

C Create and manage linked workbooks.

D Create a workspace to manage workbooks.

Topic A: Using multiple workbooks

This topic covers the following Microsoft Office Specialist objectives for exam 77-882: Excel 2010.

#	Objective
4.1	Create and format worksheets
	4.1.3 Copy worksheets

Opening and switching between multiple workbooks

Explanation

For various reasons, you might want to have more than one workbook open at a time. You can open and work with as many workbooks as your computer's memory permits. Each workbook has its own window and appears in the Excel jump list on the Windows taskbar.

To switch between workbooks, you can select the desired workbook from the Excel jump list on the taskbar. (The jump list is a new feature in Windows 7.) You can also click the View tab on the Ribbon, click Switch Windows (in the Window group), and then choose the desired workbook, as shown in Exhibit 1-1.

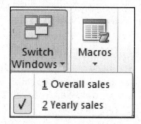

Exhibit 1-1: The Switch Windows menu on the View tab

Do it!

A-1: Switching between workbooks

The files for this activity are in Student Data folder **Unit 1\Topic A**.

Here's how	Here's why
1 Open Microsoft Excel 2010	Click Start and choose All Programs, Microsoft Office, Microsoft Excel 2010.
Close the blank workbook	
2 Open Yearly sales	On the desktop, in the Student Data\Unit 1\ Topic A folder.
Open Overall sales	You can use the Excel jump list on the taskbar to switch between open files. (Your taskbar might look different depending on the applications that are running.)
3 On the taskbar, display the Excel jump list and select **Yearly sales**	To switch to the Yearly sales workbook.
4 Click the **View** tab	On the Ribbon.
In the Window group, click **Switch Windows**	To display the list of open workbooks, as shown in Exhibit 1-1. The names of the two open workbooks appear, with a checkmark beside the active workbook.
5 Choose **Overall sales**	To switch to that workbook.
6 Close the workbook	If prompted, don't save changes.
Switch to Yearly sales and save it as **My yearly sales**	In Student Data folder Unit 1\Topic A.

Copying worksheets between workbooks

Explanation

You can copy worksheets between workbooks as easily as copying worksheets within a workbook. Be aware, however, that worksheets containing formulas or charts based on data elsewhere in that workbook might become inaccurate when moved to a new workbook.

To copy a worksheet to another workbook, make sure the target workbook is open. Then do the following:

1 Click the worksheet you want to copy.

2 On the Home tab, in the Cells group, click Format to display the Format menu.

3 Under Organize Sheets, choose Move or Copy Sheet to open the Move or Copy dialog box.

4 In the To book list, select the name of the workbook you want to copy to.

5 In the Before sheet list, either select the name of the sheet before which you want to place the copy, or select "(move to end)," as shown in Exhibit 1-2.

6 Check "Create a copy."

7 Click OK.

You can also open the Move or Copy dialog box by right-clicking the worksheet and choosing Move or Copy.

Exhibit 1-2: The Move or Copy dialog box

Do it!   **A-2: Copying a worksheet to another workbook**

The files for this activity are in Student Data folder **Unit 1\Topic A**.

Here's how	Here's why
1 Open Product	You'll copy the Product details worksheet to another workbook.
2 Click the **Home** tab	
In the Cells group, click **Format**	To display the Format menu.
Choose **Move or Copy Sheet...**	To open the Move or Copy dialog box.
3 From the To book list, select **My yearly sales**	This is the workbook to which you'll copy the worksheet.
4 In the Before sheet list, select **(move to end)**	To position the copy as the last sheet in the My yearly sales workbook.
5 Check **Create a copy**	As shown in Exhibit 1-2.
6 Click **OK**	To create the copy and place it in the new workbook. The My yearly sales workbook becomes active, showing the copy of the Product details worksheet.
7 Switch to Product	
Close the workbook	If prompted, don't save changes.
8 Update and close My yearly sales	

Topic B: Linking worksheets with 3-D formulas

Explanation   This topic covers creating 3-D formulas and using a Watch window to monitor changes in worksheet data.

Syntax of 3-D formulas

A *3-D formula* refers to the same cell or range in multiple worksheets. For example, the formula =SUM(North:West!B5) add the data in the B5 cells in the range North:West in four worksheets. The syntax for referring to cells in another worksheet is:

```
worksheet_name!reference
```

Here, `worksheet_name` refers to the name of the worksheet that provides the data, `reference` is the name of the cell or range, and `!` is the divider between the worksheet reference and the cell reference.

Inserting a 3-D reference

To insert a 3-D reference into a formula:

1   Enter the formula until the point where you need a value from another worksheet to complete the formula.

2   Click the first worksheet you want to refer to.

3   While pressing Shift, click the last worksheet you want to refer to in the formula.

4   Select the cell or range containing the values you want the formula to refer to.

5   Complete the formula and press Enter. Exhibit 1-3 shows a worksheet with 3-D formulas applied (the results of Activity B-1).

Product	Qtr1	Qtr2	Qtr3	Qtr4
Anise Seeds	$2,725	$2,114	$2,467	$2,676
Asafoetida Powder	$2,674	$2,535	$2,553	$3,208
Basil Leaf (Whole)	$29,783	$28,751	$23,478	$33,117
Bay Leaf (Whole)	$1,773	$2,780	$2,620	$2,607
Caraway Seed (Whole)	$2,263	$3,084	$2,368	$2,112
Cardamom Seed (Whole)	$1,277	$2,199	$1,618	$2,619
Cardamom Seed (Ground)	$2,489	$2,760	$2,561	$2,804
Catnip Leaf	$3,447	$1,466	$1,870	$2,950
Celery Seed (Whole)	$24,232	$28,437	$23,697	$18,124
Chamomile Flowers	$1,770	$2,591	$2,323	$2,209

Exhibit 1-3: A worksheet with 3-D formulas applied in Activity B-1

Do it!   ## B-1:   Creating 3-D formulas

The files for this activity are in Student Data folder **Unit 1\Topic B**.

Here's how	Here's why
1 Open Regions	
Save the workbook as **My regions**	
2 Click the **North** sheet	
View the South, East, and West sheets	Each worksheet contains quarterly sales figures for a different sales region.
Click the **Creating 3-D formula** sheet	
3 In B5, type **=SUM(**	To begin the function.
4 Click the **North** sheet	To select the first worksheet in the 3-D reference.
Press (SHIFT) and click the **West** sheet	To specify the worksheet range North:West in the function. The color of the four worksheet tabs in the range changes to white.
Release (SHIFT)	
5 In the active worksheet, select B5	To select the cell containing the first-quarter anise seed sales in each of the four selected worksheets.
Type **)** and press (↵ ENTER)	To complete the 3-D formula. The sheet named "Creating 3-D formula" automatically becomes the active worksheet again.
6 Select B5	In the Creating 3-D formula worksheet.
Observe the formula bar	⟨ *fx* =SUM(North:West!B5) In the formula, North:West refers to the worksheet range North through West (North, South, East, and West), ! is the divider between the worksheet and cell references, and B5 is the cell address.
7 Copy the formula in B5 to the rest of the range B5:E14	(Use the fill handle in the bottom-right corner of B5.) To calculate the total quarterly sales for each product.
8 Deselect the cells	Click anywhere in the worksheet.
9 Observe the worksheet	The worksheet should resemble Exhibit 1-3.
10 Update the workbook	

Adding a Watch window

Explanation

Excel formulas can refer to cells or ranges in other worksheets, or a range of worksheets, within a workbook. This type of formula creates a link between worksheets. When two worksheets are linked, any change you make in the source cell is automatically updated in the linked cell. You can observe this effect by adding a *Watch window* to the source cell. This way, you don't need to navigate to the other worksheets to see the updated information.

To add a Watch window:

1   Select the cell to which you want to add a Watch window.

2   Click the Formulas tab.

3   In the Formula Auditing group, click Watch Window.

4   Click Add Watch to open the Watch Window dialog box.

5   Click Add to place this cell in the Watch window.

Do it!

B-2: Adding a Watch window

Here's how	Here's why
1 Click the **Report** sheet	This worksheet contains summarized data from the North, South, East, and West worksheets. You'll add a Watch window.
Select B5	f_x =SUM(North:West!B5) B5 has the value $2,725, which is the sum of all cells with the address B5 in the worksheet range North:West. This value is the bonus first-quarter sales of anise seeds from all four regions.
2 Click the **Formulas** tab	On the Ribbon.
3 In the Formula Auditing group, click **Watch Window**	To open a Watch window.
Click **Add Watch**	**Add Watch** Select the cells that you would like to watch =Report!$B$5 To open the Add Watch dialog box. Cell B5 in the Report worksheet is automatically selected because that is the active cell.
Click **Add**	To select this cell and add it to the Watch window. The workbook, sheet, cell, value, and formula for B5 appear in the Watch window.
4 Click the **North** sheet	The Watch window remains visible, no matter which worksheet is active. You'll change the value of B5 in this worksheet and observe the change in the linked cell in the Watch window.
Observe the value in the Watch window	 | Book	Sheet	Name	Cell	Value
---	---	---	---	---
My reg...	Report		B5	$2,725	 In the Watch window, the value in B5 of the Report worksheet is $2,725.
In B5, enter **1000**	 | Book	Sheet	Name	Cell	Value
---	---	---	---	---
My reg...	Report		B5	$3,191	 The value in B5 of the Report worksheet is updated to $3,191.
5 Close the Watch window	
6 Update and close the workbook	

Topic C: Linking workbooks

Explanation

Just as you can link multiple worksheets within a workbook, you can link multiple workbooks. You can do this by writing a formula in one workbook that refers to a cell, range, or name in another workbook. References to other workbooks are called *external references*. You can maintain workbook links even if the workbook that is referred to is renamed.

External links

The syntax for referring to cells in another workbook is:

```
'[workbook_name]worksheet_name'!reference
```

Here, `workbook_name` refers to the name of the workbook that provides the data, and `worksheet_name` refers to the name of the worksheet in the source workbook. At the end of the formula, `reference` is the name of the cell or range, and `!` is the divider between the worksheet reference and the cell reference.

Security warnings

By default, Microsoft Excel 2010 is configured to prompt you when a workbook that has external links requires those links to be updated. This is a security measure that is intended to protect your workbooks from viruses and other malicious code. When you open a workbook containing external links that need updating, Excel displays a security warning, shown in Exhibit 1-4, below the Ribbon. To enable the updating of links between workbooks, click Enable Content.

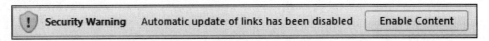

Exhibit 1-4: The security warning appears between the Ribbon and the formula bar

Do it!

C-1: Examining external links in a worksheet

The files for this activity are in Student Data folder **Unit 1\Topic C**.

Here's how	Here's why
1 Open Revenue	
Save the workbook as **My revenue**	In the current topic folder.
2 In the security warning, click **Enable Content**	(The security warning appears between the Ribbon and the formula bar.) To enable automatic updating of the workbook links. The security warning disappears.
Click **Update**	(If necessary.) To allow the automatic updating of external links.
3 Click the **Quarterly revenue** sheet	(If necessary.) This worksheet contains the quarterly revenue report for four sales regions. The workbook My revenue is linked to the Bonus sales workbook. Column C of the Quarterly revenue worksheet contains total sales for the first quarter.
Select C6	
Observe the formula bar	

f_x ='C:\Users\User01\Desktop\Student Data\Unit 1\Topic C\[Bonus sales.xlsx]North'!$B$15

	The formula bar displays the path and source of the link. (Your path might look different depending on how folders are configured on your PC.) In the formula bar, Bonus sales is the source workbook, North is the worksheet, and $B$15 is the cell address to which the formula is linked. The current value in this cell is 14,074.
4 Open the Bonus sales workbook	The North worksheet is active.
Edit B5 to read **1000**	The value in B15 changes from $14,074 to $14,540.
5 Switch to the **My revenue** workbook	To see the changes in the linked workbook. In the Quarterly revenue worksheet, the value in C6 has also changed from 14,074 to 14,540.
6 Update the workbook	

Creating external links

Explanation

When you build formulas that refer to worksheets in other workbooks, the workbook that contains the formula is called the *destination workbook*, and the workbook to which the formula refers is called the *source workbook*.

To create an external link:

1 Open the destination workbook.
2 Select the cell where you want to enter the formula.
3 Type the equals sign (=).
4 Click the source workbook.
5 Select the cell that you want the formula to refer to.
6 Press Enter.

Region	Total expenses	Total sales	Profit/Loss
North	$13,395	$62,216	$48,821
South	$89,000	$88,358	($642)
East	$21,947	$76,345	$54,398
West	$15,530	$60,678	$45,148

Exhibit 1-5: A worksheet with external references after Activity C-2

Do it!

C-2:   Creating external links in a worksheet

Here's how	Here's why
1 Click the **Total revenue** sheet	You'll create a link between the My revenue workbook and the Bonus sales workbook. The Profit/Loss column displays profit or loss data for each region. Currently, the Total sales column does not contain any data.
2 In C5, enter **=**	
Switch to the **Bonus sales** workbook	The North worksheet is active.
Select F15	f_x ='[Bonus sales.xlsx]North'!$F$15
	To enter a linked reference. Bonus sales is the workbook name, North is the worksheet name, and $F$15 is the cell reference.
Press (↵ ENTER)	To enter the external reference. The My revenue workbook becomes active. C5 shows the formula's result, which is $62,216.
3 Enter the external references for the remaining regions	(Remember to enter these as linked references.) Type the =, click the respective region tabs in the Bonus sales workbook, select the total sales value in F15, and press Enter. The worksheet will resemble Exhibit 1-5.
4 Update the workbook	

Maintaining workbook links

Explanation

You can change the name of a workbook even if it is linked to another workbook. If both the source and destination workbooks are open, the link is updated automatically. If you don't have the destination workbook open, you can still redirect the links by using the Connections group on the Data tab.

To redirect links:

1 Click the Data tab.

2 In the Connections group, click Edit Links to open the Edit Links dialog box, shown in Exhibit 1-6.

3 From the Source file list, select the source workbook whose links you want to redirect.

4 Click the Change Source button to open the Change Source dialog box.

5 Select the name of the workbook to which you want to redirect the link. Click OK to return to the Edit Links dialog box.

6 Click Close to close the Edit Links dialog box.

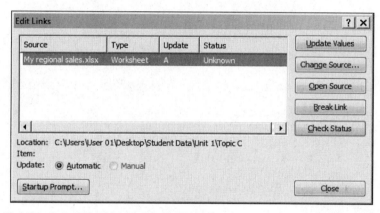

Exhibit 1-6: The Edit Links dialog box

Do it!

C-3: Editing links

The files for this activity are in Student Data folder **Unit 1\Topic C**.

Here's how	Here's why
1 Select C5	f_x ='[Bonus sales.xlsx]North'!$F$15
	(In the Total revenue worksheet in My revenue.) The formula in the formula bar contains a reference to the Bonus sales workbook.
2 Switch to the **Bonus sales** workbook	
Save the workbook as **My regional sales**	Saving the source file with a different name will automatically update the link in the destination file.
3 Switch to the **My revenue** workbook	
Select C5	f_x ='[My regional sales.xlsx]North'!$F$15
	(If necessary.) To view the updated link. The formula now contains a reference to My regional sales instead of to Bonus sales.
4 Update and close My revenue	
5 Save the My regional sales workbook as **My new regional sales**	
6 Open My revenue	You are prompted to update the links in My revenue.
Click **Enable Content**	If necessary.
Click **Update**	(If prompted.) To allow the automatic updating of external links.
7 Select C5	(If necessary.) The formula still refers to My regional sales.xlsx.
8 Click the **Data** tab	You'll edit the links to refer to another workbook.
In the Connections group, click **Edit Links**	To open the Edit Links dialog box. In Exhibit 1-6, the name of the source workbook is shown as My regional sales.xlsx.
Click **Change Source**	To open the Change Source: My regional sales.xlsx dialog box.
In the list of files, double-click **My new regional sales**	In the source list, the name of the workbook is now My new regional sales.xlsx.

9 Click **Close**

Observe the formula bar

| f_x | =`'[My new regional sales.xlsx]North'!$F$15` |

The reference to My regional sales.xlsx has changed to My new regional sales.xlsx.

10 Update My revenue

Close all open workbooks

Topic D: Managing workbooks

This topic covers the following Microsoft Office Specialist objectives for exam 77-882: Excel 2010.

#	Objective
4.2	**Manipulate window views**
	4.2.2 Arrange window views

Workspaces

Explanation

If you find that you repeatedly use the same set of workbooks, you can save them as a workspace. A *workspace* is a logical container of related workbooks that retains page setups, window sizes, and display settings. A workspace does not save the workbooks themselves, so you'll still need to save changes in each workbook individually.

While working with multiple workbooks, you can arrange them in a specific way on the screen to maximize the data you can see. To do so, on the View tab, in the Window group, click Arrange All. Select the desired Arrange option (Tiled, Horizontal, Vertical, or Cascade), and click OK.

Excel calls this arrangement a workspace. You can save this arrangement in a workspace file, which stores the position and size of the window for each open workbook. By default, Excel saves the workspace file with the name "resume." You can rename the file if you use different workspace files for different workbooks. The file extension for workspaces is .xlw.

To create a workspace:

1   Open all of the workbooks that you want to save together as a workspace.

2   Set the window sizes, screen magnifications, and any other display settings as you want them to be whenever you open the workspace.

3   Click the View tab.

4   In the Window group, click Save Workspace to open the Save Workspace dialog box.

5   Specify a name and location for the workspace, and click Save.

To open a workspace, select it from the Open dialog box.

Do it!

D-1:   Creating a workspace

The files for this activity are in Student Data folder **Unit 1\Topic D**.

Here's how	Here's why
1 Open Revenue report and save it as **My revenue report**	In Student Data folder Unit 1\Topic D.
Open Product sales and save it as **My product sales**	
2 Click the **View** tab	You'll arrange the two open workbooks and save the resulting workspace.
3 In the Window group, click **Arrange All**	To open the Arrange Windows dialog box.
Select **Vertical**	

Arrange Windows

Arrange
- ○ Tiled
- ○ Horizontal
- ● Vertical
- ○ Cascade

☐ Windows of active workbook

OK   Cancel

Click **OK**	The open workbooks are both displayed, with a vertical divider between them.
4 Click the **My revenue report** workbook	(If necessary.) Click anywhere on the worksheet.
Change the magnification to **75%**	Click the Zoom button on the taskbar and select 75% in the Zoom dialog box, or drag the slider until the Zoom button reads 75%.
5 Change the magnification for My product sales to **75%**	

6	In the Window group, click **Save Workspace**	To open the Save Workspace dialog box. By default, Workspaces is selected in the Save as type list.
	Navigate to the current topic folder	If necessary.
	Observe the default name in the File name box	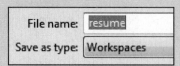 The default file name is "resume" and the file type is Workspaces.
	Edit the File name box to read **My sales**	
7	Click **Save**	To save the workspace. If a message box asks if you want to save workbook changes, click Save.
8	Close all open workbooks	
9	Display the Open dialog box	
	Select **My sales**	
	Click **Open**	The workbooks My revenue report and My product sales appear, just as they did when you saved the workspace.
10	Open Quarters	You'll add another workbook to the workspace.
11	Open the Arrange Windows dialog box	In the Window group, click Arrange All.
	Select **Tiled** and click **OK**	To tile the open windows and close the dialog box.
12	Open the Save Workspace dialog box	(Click the View tab and click Save Workspace.) In the File name box, My sales is selected.
	Click **Save**	A message box asks if you want to replace the existing workspace.
	Click **Yes**	If a message box asks if you want to save workbook changes, click Save.
13	Close all open workbooks	
14	Open My sales	The three workbooks appear as they did when you saved the workspace.
15	Close all open workbooks	If you're prompted to save changes, click Don't Save.

File name: resume
Save as type: Workspaces

Unit summary: Using multiple worksheets and workbooks

Topic A   In this topic, you **switched** between open workbooks and **copied** a worksheet from one workbook to another.

Topic B   In this topic, you created **3-D formulas** to perform calculations across multiple worksheets. You also learned that Excel automatically updates the data in destination cells if you change the data in the source cells. You observed this in the **Watch window** without navigating between worksheets.

Topic C   In this topic, you created **external links** to data in another workbook. You learned that data is automatically updated in the destination workbook when you change the data in the source workbook. You also used the **Edit Links** dialog box to change links in destination workbooks.

Topic D   In this topic, you saved the display settings of several workbooks as a **workspace**, making it easier to open and work on them simultaneously.

Independent practice activity

In this activity, you will create 3-D formulas and create and update external links. You'll open multiple workbooks, arrange them in a workspace, and save the workspace.

The files for this activity are in Student Data folder **Unit 1\Unit summary**.

1 Open Practice sales and save it as **My practice sales**. Open Product details and save it as **My product details**. (You might need to maximize the windows.)

2 Click the Report worksheet in the My practice sales workbook.

3 Create 3-D formulas to calculate the total sales (in $) for all products in all four regions. The formula for calculating total sales is **Qty Sold * Price**. Qty Sold for each region is stored in the respective region worksheets of the My Practice sales workbook. Prices are stored in the My product workbook.

   To do this for the North region, in My practice sales, click Report and type = in B5. In My product details, select C5. In the formula bar, make the reference to C5 relative by removing the $ signs before C and 5. Then, type * after C5 in the formula bar. Click the North tab in My practice sales, select B5, and press Enter. Use AutoFill to obtain the values for the rest of the Products under North.

   Using the same technique, create formulas for C5:E5, and use AutoFill to obtain the values for the remaining regions and products. When you're done, compare your results with Exhibit 1-7.

4 Update and close My practice sales. Close My product details.

5 Open the Quarterly sales workbook. Open Total revenue and save it as **My total revenue**. Click the Quarterly revenue worksheet in the My total revenue workbook. Verify that the Quarterly revenue worksheet is linked to the Quarterly sales workbook.

6 Change the name of the Quarterly sales workbook to **My annual sales**. (Save the workbook with the new name.)

7 Verify that the source of the link is updated in the My total revenue workbook.

8 Arrange the open workbooks horizontally in the Excel window.

9 Create a workspace named **My practice sales** that saves the current display settings.

10 Update and close both workbooks.

	A	B	C	D	E
1		**Outlander Spices**			
2		**Bonus sales for all regions**			
3					
4	Product	North	South	East	West
5	Cassia	$5,372,210	$2,773,022	$2,646,600	$5,025,112
6	Catnip Leaf	$5,861,990	$1,218,444	$3,025,701	$2,747,250
7	Celery Seed (Whole)	$383,650	$677,865	$328,505	$909,246
8	Celery Seed (Ground)	$4,198,897	$2,614,144	$4,363,487	$3,265,665
9	Chamomile Flowers	$69,156	$286,677	$492,055	$253,669
10	Chili Pepper Powder	$2,266,212	$5,544,111	$4,082,834	$2,125,811
11	Chinese Star Anise (Ground)	$1,922,761	$4,358,487	$2,488,171	$473,145
12	Chinese Star Anise (Whole)	$697,750	$7,128,062	$931,406	$4,509,601
13	Chives	$7,725,468	$4,092,269	$2,398,023	$448,908
14	Cilantro Flakes	$7,938,853	$2,884,557	$1,442,793	$1,953,937

Exhibit 1-7: A sample of the My practice sales workbook after Step 3

Review questions

1 What is a 3-D formula?

2 What is the advantage of a Watch window?

3 How do you redirect a workbook link?

4 What is a workspace?

5 When you save a workspace, are the workbooks themselves also saved individually?

Unit 2

Advanced formatting

Unit time: 75 minutes

Complete this unit, and you'll know how to:

A Apply built-in and custom number formats to display data in specific formats.

B Use the UPPER, LOWER, PROPER, and SUBSTITUTE functions to modify text.

C Create, apply, and modify styles to apply several kinds of formatting simultaneously.

D Apply and modify themes.

E Merge and change orientation of cells to display text in special ways; transpose data; and add backgrounds and watermarks

Topic A: Using special number formats

This topic covers the following Microsoft Office Specialist objectives for exam 77-882: Excel 2010.

#	Objective
1.3	**Personalize the environment by using Backstage**
	1.3.3 Manipulate Excel default settings (Excel Options)
3.1	**Apply and modify cell formats**
	3.1.2 Apply a number format

This topic covers the following Microsoft Office Specialist objectives for exam 77-888: Excel Expert 2010.

#	Objective
1.1	**Apply workbook settings, properties, and data options**
	1.1.1 Set advanced properties

Built-in and custom formats

Explanation

You can apply special number formats—such as ZIP codes and phone numbers—to change the appearance of numerical information. You can do this by using built-in formats or creating your own formats. You can also show or hide zeros in the worksheet.

When you apply a special number format to data in your worksheets, Excel changes only the cell's appearance and not the cell's value. So, when you click a cell where a number format has been applied, the formula bar still displays the unformatted value. Exhibit 2-1 shows part of a worksheet where built-in number formats have been applied to ZIP codes and phone numbers.

To apply a special format:

1   Open the Format Cells dialog box and click the Number tab.

2   In the Category list, select Special, as shown in Exhibit 2-2.

3   In the Type list, select a format type. Click OK.

City	Zip code	Name	Phone number
Ashford	06278	Bill MacArthur	(907) 555-4024
Georgetown	80444	Jamie Morrison	(800) 555-5425
Elbert	80106	Maureen O'Connor	(520) 555-0767
Farmington	06032	Rebecca Austin	(635) 555-4581
North Franklin	06254	Paul Anderson	(357) 555-2978
North Grosvenordale	06255	Cynthia Roberts	(526) 555-2440
North Windham	06256	Rita Greg	(246) 555-6657

Exhibit 2-1: The Number formats worksheet with special formats applied to two columns

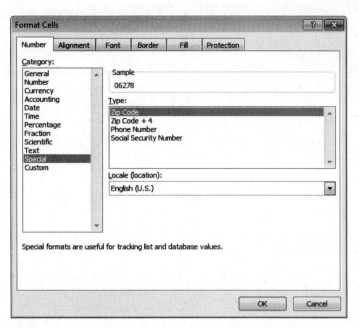

Exhibit 2-2: The Number tab in the Format Cells dialog box

Do it!

A-1:   Applying special formats

The files for this activity are in Student Data folder **Unit 2\Topic A**.

Here's how	Here's why
1 Open Managers	
Save the workbook as **My managers**	In Student Data folder Unit 2\Topic A.
2 Verify that the Number formats worksheet is active	This worksheet contains award details for managers.
3 Select B5:B23	The ZIP code column contains four- and five-digit ZIP codes. You'll apply the Zip Code format to this range to make sure that all ZIP codes contain five digits.
4 On the Home tab, in the Number group, click ⌐	(The Dialog Box Launcher button.) To open the Format Cells dialog box. The Number tab is active because you opened the dialog box from within the Number group.
In the Category list, select **Special**	The Special category includes formats for ZIP codes, phone numbers, and Social Security numbers. In the Type list, Zip Code is selected, as shown in Exhibit 2-2.
Click **OK**	To close the dialog box and apply the format.
5 Deselect the cells	The ZIP code values have been reformatted. Each four-digit value now begins with zero so that the value will conform to ZIP-code format.
6 Apply the **Phone Number** format to D5:D23	Select the range. In the Number group, click the Dialog Box Launcher to open the Format Cells dialog box with the Number tab active. In the Category list, select Special; then select Phone Number and click OK.
7 Select D5	
Observe the formula bar	*fx* 9075554024
	The cell value remains the same even though you have changed its display format in the worksheet.
8 Update the workbook	

Zero values

Explanation

Excel displays all zero values in a worksheet by default. However, if you prefer, you can hide zero values. To do so:

1   Click the File tab and choose Options.
2   Select Advanced.
3   Under "Display options for this worksheet," clear "Show a zero in cells that have zero value."
4   Click OK.

Do it!

A-2:   Controlling the display of zero values

Here's how	Here's why
1 Observe the worksheet	The Excellence awards and Gold medals columns contain several zero values.
2 Click the **File** tab	On the Ribbon.
Choose **Options**	To open the Excel Options dialog box.
In the category list, select **Advanced**	
3 Under "Display options for this worksheet," clear the indicated option	
	To hide zero values in this worksheet.
Click **OK**	To close the Excel Options dialog box.
4 Observe F5:G23	The cells that contained zero values earlier are now blank.
5 Update the workbook	

Display options for this worksheet: Number formats
☑ Show row and column headers
☐ Show formulas in cells instead of their calculated results
☐ Show sheet right-to-left
☐ Show page breaks
☐ Show a zero in cells that have zero value

Custom number formats

Explanation

In Excel, you can create custom formats in which you specify the appearance of positive numbers, negative numbers, zero values, and text data.

To create a custom number format:

1 Open the Format Cells dialog box and click the Number tab.
2 In the Category list, select Custom, as shown in Exhibit 2-3.
3 In the Type box, enter the desired format code.
4 Click OK to apply the format.

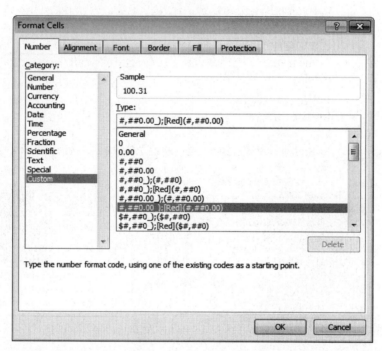

Exhibit 2-3: The Custom category on the Number tab in the Formatting Cells dialog box

A custom *format code* contains four sections—positives, negatives, zeros, and text—separated by semicolons. The syntax for all format codes is:

```
positive;negative;zero;text
```

The first section specifies how a positive value will be displayed in a cell. In the negative section, you can specify how a negative value should be displayed. The zero section controls the display of zero values, and the text section controls the display of text data. You can skip a section by entering consecutive semicolons.

Here's an example:

```
#,###.00_);[Red](#,###.00);0.00;"text"@
```

The # and 0 (zero) symbols are placeholders for digits. By using these symbols, you can specify how a numeric value should be displayed in a cell. Exhibit 2-4 shows the effects of some of these format codes.

- In the positive section of the example, the code #,###.00 means that positive numbers should have a comma in every thousandths position and have two digits after the decimal point.

- The underscore (_) adds a space that's the width of the character following it. In the example, negative numbers are enclosed in parentheses. Therefore, in the positive section, the underscore is followed by a closing parenthesis so that the positive numbers line up correctly with the negative numbers.

- In the negative section, [Red] indicates that all negative values will be displayed in the color red.

- In the zero section, 0.00 means that any zeros in the range will be shown in that format.

- The at symbol (@) displays a text value in a cell. You can identify specific text to be added automatically at the beginning of a text value; to do so, enclose that text in double quotes before the @ symbol.

Name	City	Emp #	Gold medals	Last year	This year	% Increase
Bill MacArthur	Ashford	Empl: 17-111	1	$67,678	$135,567	100.31
Jamie Morrison	Georgetown	Empl: 46-721		$76,576	$65,737	(14.15)
Jim Adams	Elbert	Empl: 42-499		$114,867	$114,688	(0.16)
Rebecca Austin	Farmington	Empl: 42-617		$76,357	$86,548	13.35
Paul Anderson	North Franklin	Empl: 46-110		$85,566	$89,076	4.10
Cynthia Roberts	North Grosvenordale	Empl: 13-330		$39,076	$56,546	44.71
Rita Greg	North Windham	Empl: 42-220		$78,678	$67,888	(13.71)
Trevor Johnson	Elizabeth	Empl: 13-631		$64,874	$87,688	35.17
Kevin Meyers	Franktown	Empl: 46-551	3	$85,559	$184,888	116.09
Adam Long	Bennett	Empl: 13-668		$75,770	$85,665	13.06
Kendra James	Quinebaug	Empl: 13-235		$65,578	$55,786	(14.93)
Michael Lee	Rogers	Empl: 42-985		$69,867	$78,798	12.78
Sandra Lawrence	Scotland	Empl: 46-330	1	$76,377	$129,867	70.03
Mary Smith	South Willington	Empl: 46-910		$75,786	$98,566	30.06
James Overmire	South Windham	Empl: 46-344		$56,587	$78,979	39.57
Annie Philips	South Woodstock	Empl: 13-241		$78,698	$65,789	(16.40)
Shannon Lee	Stonington	Empl: 13-221		$68,985	$89,089	29.14
Roger Williams	Storrs Mansfield	Empl: 42-271		$75,677	$87,588	15.74
Melissa James	Thompson	Empl: 13-216	1	$85,386	$10,984	(87.14)

Exhibit 2-4: The Custom format worksheet after custom formats have been applied

A-3:   Creating custom formats

Here's how	Here's why
1 Click the **Custom format** sheet	This worksheet contains performance details for managers. You'll make the values in the % Increase column easier to interpret.
2 Select G5:G23	These cells contain positive and negative values.
Open the Format Cells dialog box	(Click the Dialog Box Launcher in the Number group.) The Number tab is active.
3 In the Category list, select **Custom**	To display the types of custom formats available.
In the Type list, select **#,##0.00_);[Red](#,##0.00)** as shown in Exhibit 2-3	
Click **OK**	To close the dialog box and apply the format.
4 Deselect the range	The values in the % Increase column are rounded to two decimal places. Negative values appear in red.
5 Select D5:D23	You'll hide the zeros in the Gold medals column.
6 Open the Format Cells dialog box	
In the Category list, select **Custom**	
Edit the Type box to read **0;-0;;@**	(This format is not in the Type list, so you must enter it in the Type box.) Here, ";;" indicates that the zeros section in the format code is empty; therefore, zeros will not be displayed. The @ symbol specifies that the cells in the range can accept and display text values.
Click **OK**	The cells containing zero values are now blank.
7 Select C5:C23	You'll add a prefix to all values in this column and hyphenate the values.
8 Open the Format Cells dialog box and select the **Custom** category	
9 Edit the Type box to read **"Empl: "00-000**	
Click **OK**	The prefix "Empl:", followed by a space, appears before all values in the Employee number column.
10 Update and close the workbook	

Topic B: Using functions to format text

This topic covers the following Microsoft Office Specialist objectives for exam 77-882: Excel 2010.

#	Objective
2.1	Construct cell data
	2.1.1 Use Paste Special
	2.1.1.3 Values

This topic covers the following Microsoft Office Specialist objectives for exam 77-888: Excel Expert 2010.

#	Objective
2.4	Apply functions in formulas
	2.4.7 Use Text functions

The PROPER, UPPER, and LOWER functions

Explanation

In Excel, you can use a function to format text in a cell and copy the result to a range of cells. This is more efficient than manually formatting each cell individually. For example, let's say you wanted to make all names in a contact list uppercase. You could manually edit each name, but it would be much easier to use the UPPER function and copy the result to the cells you wanted to change.

Text-formatting functions include, but are not limited to, UPPER, LOWER, and PROPER. The syntax for these three functions is similar. It's the function name followed by (text), like this—

```
UPPER(text)
```

—where text is the text you want to convert. It can refer to a cell or a text string.

Do it!

B-1: Using PROPER, UPPER, and LOWER

The files for this activity are in Student Data folder **Unit 2\Topic B**.

Here's how	Here's why
1 Open Shirts	
Save the workbook as **My shirts**	In the current topic folder.
Click the **Text functions** sheet	You'll apply functions to format the text in this worksheet.
2 Select H4	
Enter **=PROPER(A4)**	To designate the text in A4 as the text you want to capitalize. Proper nouns, which include people's names, are generally capitalized.
Observe the screen	The first and last names in A4 now also appear in H4, but with each name starting with a capital letter.
3 Copy the formula in H4 to H5:H21	(Use the fill handle.) All names in the first column are capitalized.
4 Copy H4:H21	(Right-click the selection and choose Copy.) You'll paste the results of the function into the Name column.
Select A4:A21	
5 Display the Paste menu	
Under Paste Values, point to **Values**	The Paste Preview feature displays the result of pasting only the values in A4:A21.
Click	To paste only the values, not the formulas. The list is replaced with capitalized names.

6 Press (ESC)	To delete the marquee around H4:H21.
Delete the values in H4:H21	You'll use this column to convert text in other columns.
7 Select H4	
Enter **=UPPER(F4)**	To convert the text in F4 to uppercase.
8 Copy the formula in H4 to H5:H21	
Replace the values in F4:F21 with the values in H4:H21	Copy the values in H4:H21 to F4:F21, using the Paste Special command.
Delete the contents of H4:H21	
9 Convert the text in G4:G21 to lowercase	Use the LOWER function. Be sure to delete the values from H4:H21 when you're done.
10 Update the workbook	

The SUBSTITUTE function

Explanation

You can use the SUBSTITUTE function when you want to replace one character or set of characters with another set. The syntax for the SUBSTITUTE function is:

```
SUBSTITUTE(text,old_text,new_text,instance_num)
```

In this syntax, `text` is the text or cell reference for which you want to substitute new characters; `old_text` lists the characters you want to replace; and `new_text` is the text you want to substitute. `Instance_num` specifies which occurrence of `old_text` you want to replace with `new_text`.

Do it!

B-2: Using SUBSTITUTE

Here's how	Here's why
1 Observe the names in the Name column	Some letters in the last names should be capitalized, as in "MacArthur." You'll use SUBSTITUTE to correct this.
2 Select H4	
Enter the following code: `=SUBSTITUTE(A4,"a","A",2)`	In this function, A4 is the cell containing the text to be replaced; "a" is the character to be replaced; and "A" is the replacement character. The 2 refers to the occurrence of the text to be replaced—that is, the second "a" in "Macarthur."
3 Copy the value from H4 to A4	Use the Paste Special command to copy only the value in H4, not the formula.
4 In H4, enter the following code: `=SUBSTITUTE(A6,"g","G",1)`	To correct Melinda's McGregor's last name.
Copy the value to A6	
5 Delete the contents of H4	
Update and close the workbook	

Topic C: Working with styles

This topic covers the following Microsoft Office Specialist objectives for exam 77-882: Excel 2010.

#	Objective
3.6	**Create and apply cell styles**
	3.6.1 Apply cell styles
	3.6.2 Construct new cell styles

Creating and applying styles

Explanation

You might want to apply several formats at the same time. You can do this efficiently by creating a style that has all the formats you want to use and then applying that style to the cell or range. A *style* is a named collection of formats that are saved and applied as a group.

Excel provides a gallery of built-in cell styles, also called Quick Styles. You can also create and modify your own styles to make data be displayed exactly as you want.

Built-in styles

You can view a gallery of built-in styles by clicking Cell Styles in the Styles group on the Home tab. When you point to a style in the gallery, the Live Preview function temporarily applies that style to whatever cell or range is selected. If you click a style, it is applied to the selected cell, and the gallery closes. The Cell Styles gallery is shown in Exhibit 2-5.

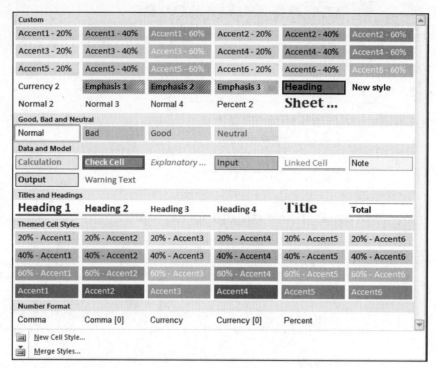

Exhibit 2-5: The Cell Styles gallery

Custom styles

You can also create your own styles that combine formats in any way you want. To create a custom style:

1   Select a cell that already has the combination of formats you want to include in the new style.

2   Click the Home tab.

3   In the Styles group, click Cell Styles to display the gallery.

4   Choose New Cell Style (near the bottom of the gallery) to open the Style dialog box, shown in Exhibit 2-6. The dialog box shows the combination of formats from the selected cell.

5   In the Style name box, enter a name for the new style.

6   Click OK to define the new style and close the dialog box.

After you create a style, the Style gallery will be divided into Custom and Built-In styles. The style you created will appear in the Custom section, near the top of the gallery.

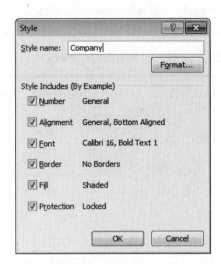

Exhibit 2-6: The Style dialog box showing the new style, Company

Do it!

C-1: Creating and applying styles

The files for this activity are in Student Data folder **Unit 2\Topic C**.

Here's how	Here's why
1 Open Performance	
Save the workbook as **My performance**	In the current topic folder.
Click the **Custom format** sheet	You'll use Live Preview to view some built-in styles; then you'll create custom styles.
Select B13	
2 In the Styles group, click **Cell Styles**	To display the Cell Styles gallery. The gallery contains only built-in styles at this time.
In the Cell Styles gallery, point as shown	
	(In the Data and Model group.) B13 changes to show the Note style, with yellow shading.
Point to the other styles in the gallery	To see Live Preview temporarily apply the styles to B13.
3 Select A1	You'll create a style based on the format of A1.
Click **Cell Styles**	To display the Cell Styles gallery.
Choose **New Cell Style...**	To open the Style dialog box.
4 Edit the Style name box to read **Company**	To name the new style, as shown in Exhibit 2-6. Under Style Includes (By Example), the formatting options of the new style are checked. These are drawn from the format of the selected cell (A1).
Click **OK**	To finish creating the Company style and close the dialog box.
5 Select G6	You'll create a style based on the format of G6.
6 Open the Style dialog box	In the Styles group, click Cell Styles; then choose New Cell Style.
Edit the Style name box to read **NegativeNum**	
Under Style Includes (By Example), clear **Border**	To ensure that the style, when applied, does not change the borders of the target cell(s).
Click **OK**	To create the NegativeNum style and close the dialog box.

7	Create a style named **ColumnHeading** based on A4	Select the cell. In the Styles group, click Cell Styles; then choose New Cell Style. Edit the Style name box to read ColumnHeading and click OK.
8	Create a style named **Title2** based on A2	The gallery already has a Title style.
9	Click the **Styles** sheet	You'll apply the styles you created to the data in this worksheet.
10	Select A1:C1	
11	Open the Cell Styles gallery	(In the Styles group, click Cell Styles.) There is now a Custom group at the top of the gallery.
	Under Custom, select **Company**	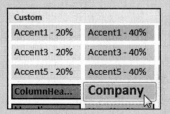
		To apply the new style to the selected range. A1:C1 has been reformatted.
12	Apply the **Title2** style to A2:C2	Open the Cell Styles gallery and select Title2.
13	Apply the **Column heading** style to A4:E4	
14	Apply the **NegativeNum** style to E5:E23	
15	Update the workbook	

Modifying built-in or custom styles

Explanation

To modify a style (built-in or custom):

1 Open the Cell Styles gallery and point to the style you want to modify.

2 Right-click and choose Modify to open the Style dialog box.

3 Clear the checkboxes for any formats you want to remove from the style.

4 If you want to add or change formats, then click Format to open the Format Cells dialog box. Make your changes and click OK.

5 Click OK to close the Style dialog box.

Do it!

C-2:   Modifying styles

Here's how	Here's why
1 Select E5	If necessary.
2 Open the Cell Styles gallery	You'll modify the NegativeNum style you created earlier.
Right-click **NegativeNum** and choose **Modify…**	To open the Style dialog box. Under Style includes, the checked boxes indicate the formats that make up this style.
Click **Format**	To open the Format Cells dialog box. You can use this dialog box to modify any style (built-in or custom).
3 Click the **Number** tab	If necessary.
Under Category, select **Number**	If necessary.
4 Edit the Decimal places box to read **1**	To specify that values displayed with the NegativeNum style will have only one digit to the right of the decimal point.
In the Negative numbers list, verify that the first format is selected	![Decimal places: 1; ✓ Use 1000 Separator (,); Negative numbers: -1,234.0 / 1,234.0 / (1,234.0) / (1,234.0)] You want to change only the number of decimal places. The NegativeNum style will still appear in black, preceded by a minus (-) sign.
Click **OK**	To close the Format Cells dialog box and return to the Style dialog box.
5 Click **OK**	To close the Style dialog box and apply the modified NegativeNum style.
6 Observe E5:E23	All cells in this range use the NegativeNum style. The values in this range now appear with only one decimal place. Negative numbers appear in black, preceded by a minus (-) sign.
7 Update and close the workbook	

Topic D: Working with themes

Explanation

At times, you might want to change some of the colors or fonts you've used in a workbook, or even in several workbooks. You could change elements individually in each sheet, but that would be tedious and time-consuming. Instead, you can use Excel's themes to swap each instance of a specific color or font with another or to quickly replace the entire color scheme.

Theme colors

When you apply colors in Excel, you can use theme colors, standard colors, recently used colors, or any color you specify, as shown in Exhibit 2-7.

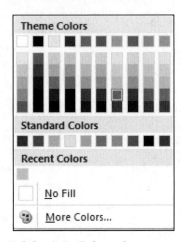

Exhibit 2-7: Color selection options

Choosing colors from the Theme Colors section of the gallery has several benefits:

- You can switch to a different theme to replace all of the theme colors at once. A theme change applies to all sheets within a workbook.

- Colors in built-in themes were selected to work harmoniously. It's easy to select complementary colors from the theme colors, whereas selecting custom colors can result in clashing combinations.

- If you apply the first four Text/Background colors—with dark text on light backgrounds, and light text on dark backgrounds—for their intended purposes, and then switch themes, the text will probably still be legible regardless of the theme you change to. All of the default themes that come with Office 2010 position the dark and light colors in the same positions within the theme. So, a theme change could switch from white text on dark blue to very light gray text on dark green—but not to navy blue text on black, which would be hard to read.

- Each theme color appears in several *tints*, or brightness variations. For a simple but effective look, you can juxtapose light and dark tints of the same color (for example, placing dark blue text in a cell filled with light blue).

Applying themes

In addition to controlling colors, each theme also controls fonts and effects. You can switch all of these attributes at once, or change just one of them.

To swap multiple colors, fonts, or effects by using themes:

1   Apply colors with the possibility of changing themes in mind:

- Apply theme colors wherever you anticipate needing to change colors globally (throughout a workbook). Many built-in cell styles are formatted with theme colors for consistency.

- For the most reliable text legibility when switching themes, use the first four colors for text and backgrounds, with contrasting combinations (light on dark or vice versa).

- If you want certain colors *not* to change (for example, fill colors in cells you want to draw attention to), then use either standard colors or colors you define yourself, not theme colors.

2   Click the Page Layout tab.

3   Change one or more theme attributes:

- To change colors, fonts, and effects all at once, select a theme from the Themes gallery in the Themes group.

- To change colors, fonts, or effects individually, choose options from the corresponding menus in the Themes group.

Do it!

D-1: Changing to a different theme

The files for this activity are in Student Data folder **Unit 2\Topic D**.

Here's how	Here's why
1 Open Comparison report	
Save the workbook as **My comparison report**	You'll apply formatting with both theme and non-theme colors.
2 Select A2	You'll apply a cell style that uses a theme color.
3 Open the Cell Styles gallery	
Under Titles and Headings, select **Heading 1**	To apply the Heading 1 style.
Observe the font color applied	(Click the Font Color gallery in the Font group and observe the color with the box around it.) This text has been formatted with the Dark Blue, Text 2 color.
4 From the Fill Color gallery in the Font group, select the indicated color	To apply an accent color that will change when you change themes. You'll select some contrasting type and background colors for the table headings and body.
5 Select B4:F4	
Hold CTRL and select A5:A9	To select the two non-contiguous ranges simultaneously.
In the Fill Color gallery, select **Dark Blue, Text 2**	The non-contiguous ranges are now filled with dark blue color.
In the Font Color gallery, select **White, Background 1**	(In the Font group.) To create contrasting text for the dark background.
6 Select B5:F9	The values in the table.
In the Fill Color gallery, select **Tan, Background 2**	To fill the table body with a light color. Next, you'll highlight a cell that represents good growth from the prior year.

7 Fill D9 with a green color under Standard colors	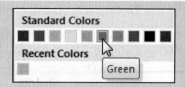
	To apply a contrasting color that won't change when you change themes.
Click the **Profit projection** sheet	To observe that this sheet was already formatted with many of the same colors. You'll switch themes to change the entire color scheme for both sheets in one step.
8 Click the **Page Layout** tab	
9 In the Themes group, click **Themes**	To open the Themes gallery.
10 Point to several themes to see the effect on the colors and fonts in the worksheet	Colors and fonts change to reflect the colors and fonts each theme would apply.
11 Point to the Civic theme	The table text remains legible, but the text in A2 is harder to read. This step demonstrates that the Text/Background color choices are safe for legibility when you change themes, but type over accent colors might be hard to read when another theme is applied.
12 Select the Origin theme	This theme applies muted, conservative colors and fonts typically appropriate for financial reporting. However, the red color in B9 remains because it is a standard color, not a theme color.
13 Click the **Sales report** sheet	The colors were applied to all sheets in the workbook. The green color you applied to D9 remains because it is not a theme color.
14 Update the workbook	

Defining theme colors

Explanation

In addition to applying themes in their entirety, you can use the Create New Theme Colors dialog box, shown in Exhibit 2-8, to define your own sets of colors. You can save just the colors, or an entire new theme, to create a formatting scheme that fits your organization's identity.

Exhibit 2-8: The Create New Theme Colors dialog box

To create a new set of theme colors:

1 Click the Page Layout tab.
2 In the Themes group, from the Colors menu, choose Create New Theme Colors.
3 Change one or more of the theme colors. To do so, click the button for the color you want to change, and then do one of the following:

   • Select one of the other theme colors (although this would create some redundant colors in the palette).
   • Select one of the standard colors.
   • Click More Colors to open the Colors dialog box, and use it to select or define a color from millions of possibilities.

4 In the Name box, enter a name for the new set of theme colors.
5 Click Save.

Changing and saving other theme attributes

You can also change a theme's fonts and effects. Select fonts and effects from the lists in the Themes dialog box to apply them to the current workbook.

To save the current combination of colors, fonts, and effects as a theme, choose Save Current Theme from the Themes menu, enter a name, and click Save.

Do it!   **D-2:   Saving new colors and themes**

Here's how	Here's why
1 In the Themes group, from the Colors gallery, choose **Create New Theme Colors...**	To open the Create New Theme Colors dialog box. You'll change the third Text/Background color to a dark blue to give the workbook a bit more color.
Click as shown	Theme colors Text/Background - Dark 1 ▼ Text/Background - Light 1 ▼ Text/Background - Dark 2 ▼ Text/Background - Light 2 ▼ To display the palette for the Text/Background - Dark 2 theme color.
In the Standard colors, select **Dark Blue**	**Standard Colors** More Colors... Dark Blue The second-to-last color.
2 Edit the Name box to read **My colors**	
Click **Save**	To close the dialog box and save the new theme colors. The text in the top two cells and in the table heading cells is dark blue because those cells are formatted with the Text/Background - Dark 2 color.
3 In the Themes group, open the Colors gallery	You'll modify the theme colors you just created.
Under Custom, right-click **My colors**	Colors ▼ **Custom** My colors ize Pri **Built-In** Edit... To display a shortcut menu.
Choose **Edit...**	To open the Edit Theme Colors dialog box.
4 Click the arrow to the right of Text/Background - Dark 2	To display the color palette.
Choose **More Colors...**	To open the Colors dialog box.

5 Click the **Custom** tab	(If necessary.) To display a more versatile interface for selecting colors than the Standard tab provides. Colors are represented numerically as amounts of Red, Green, and Blue (RGB) components. Each component can range in value from 0 (none of that component) to 255 (that component fully saturated). The higher the RGB component values, the brighter the color overall.
6 Drag the Brightness slider up until the Green value is approximately 50 and the Blue value is approximately 150, as shown	

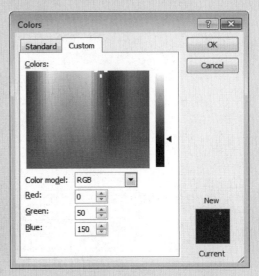

7 Click **OK**	To close the Colors dialog box.
Click **Save**	To close the Edit Theme Colors dialog box and save the set of colors. Next, you'll change the default heading and body fonts.
8 In the Themes group, display the Fonts menu and choose **Flow**	To select a combination of Heading and Body fonts. These appear in the top two cells in this worksheet because the Sheet Title and Heading 1 cell styles specify the Heading and Body fonts.
9 From the Themes menu, choose **Save Current Theme...**	To open the Save Current Theme dialog box.
In the File name box, enter **My theme**	The file type is Office Theme. You can use this new theme in other Office files.
Click **Save**	
10 In the Themes gallery, select another theme	(Any theme will do.) To change the formatting.
From the Themes menu, under Custom, choose **My theme**	To reapply your formatting to the cells that use theme colors and fonts.
11 Update and close the workbook	

Topic E: Other advanced formatting

This topic covers the following Microsoft Office Specialist objectives for exam 77-882: Excel 2010.

#	Objective
2.1	**Construct cell data**
	2.1.1 Use Paste Special
	2.1.1.4 Preview icons
	2.1.1.5 Transpose rows
	2.1.1.6 Transpose columns
	2.1.1.7 Operations
3.1	**Apply and modify cell formats**
	3.1.3 Wrapping text in a cell
3.2	**Merge or split cells**
	3.2.1 Use Merge & Center
	3.2.2 Merge Across
	3.2.3 Merge cells
	3.2.4 Unmerge cells

Merging cells

Explanation

You can change the appearance of text in a worksheet in a variety of ways. You can merge cells, center cells, and use indents to align text within cells or within text boxes. When text extends across multiple cells, you can merge the cells into a single cell. On the Home tab, in the Alignment group, click the arrow on the Merge & Center button and choose one of the following options:

- **Merge & Center** — Use to merge cells in a column or a row and to horizontally center the text. You can use the vertical and horizontal alignment buttons in the Alignment group to change the position of text in a merged cell.

- **Merge Across** — Use to merge the cells in the same row without centering the cell content.

- **Merge Cells** — Use to merge cells from multiple rows and columns into a single large cell.

Do it!

E-1: Merging cells

The files for this activity are in Student Data folder **Unit 2\Topic E**.

Here's how	Here's why
1 Open Sales report	
Save the workbook as **My sales report**	In the current topic folder.
Click the **Sales** sheet	You'll insert a table title in this worksheet.
2 Insert a column before column A	(Select column A, right-click, and choose Insert.) An Insert Options button appears.
3 Select A5	
Enter **East and North regions**	The text is not completely visible.
4 Click the **Home** tab	If necessary.
5 Select A5:A17	
In the Alignment group, click the arrow next to Merge & Center	
	To display the Merge & Center menu.
Choose **Merge Cells**	The cells have been merged into one cell, but the text is still not completely visible. The text appears centered at the bottom of the cell. You'll correct this in the next activity.
6 Observe the heading text above the table	With the new column added, the heading isn't centered.
Select C2:E3	You can use the Merge Across feature to merge each heading at the same time.
From the Merge & Center menu, choose **Merge Across**	
	Both headings are merged in their respective rows.
7 Update the workbook	

Wrapping text

Explanation

When a cell contains more text than is visible, you can *wrap the text* to fit within the cell and appear on multiple lines. The cell width remains the same, but the cell height changes to accommodate the text.

To wrap text in a selected cell, click the Wrap Text button in the Alignment group on the Home tab.

Changing the orientation of cell contents

You can change the orientation of text in a cell, as shown in Exhibit 2-9. *Orientation* refers to the direction of text flow in a cell. By default, text is horizontal. You can also display it vertically or rotate it to a specific angle.

To do this, use the Orientation button in the Alignment group on the Home tab. To rotate text to a specific angle, open the Format Cells dialog box and enter a value between 0 and 90 degrees in the Degrees box on the Alignment tab. A preview of the angle is displayed for you.

	Product	Region	January	February	March	April	Total
	Cinnamon (Ground Korintje)	East	$20,345	$29,196	$17,990	$18,158	$85,689
	Cinnamon (Ground) Extra High Oil (2X)	East	$26,400	$34,879	$15,541	$22,731	$99,551
	Anise Seeds	East	$2,253	$2,139	$11,312	$20,218	$35,923
	Annatto Seed	East	$2,146	$1,871	$11,771	$24,181	$39,969
East and North regions	Asafoetida Powder	East	$18,772	$18,780	$19,426	$23,273	$80,251
	Sub total (East)		$69,916	$86,865	$76,039	$108,561	$341,381
	Basil Leaf (Whole)	North	$2,511	$2,158	$17,611	$25,166	$47,446
	Basil Leaf (Ground)	North	$3,829	$1,753	$17,314	$17,924	$40,820
	Cardamom Seed (Ground)	North	$3,190	$2,471	$17,975	$25,573	$49,209
	Carob Powder (Raw)	North	$3,248	$3,253	$13,839	$18,336	$38,676
	Carob Pods (Ribbled)	North	$2,301	$2,468	$17,648	$23,818	$46,235
	Sub total (North)		$15,079	$12,103	$84,388	$110,817	$222,387

Exhibit 2-9: Text in the first column is rotated up

Do it!

E-2:   Changing the orientation of text in a cell

Here's how	Here's why
1 Select A5	You'll change the orientation of text in the cell so that the title is completely visible.
2 In the Alignment group, click [🗐 Wrap Text]	<table><tr><td>5</td><td></td></tr><tr><td>6</td><td></td></tr><tr><td>7</td><td></td></tr><tr><td>8</td><td></td></tr><tr><td>9</td><td></td></tr><tr><td>10</td><td></td></tr><tr><td>11</td><td></td></tr><tr><td>12</td><td></td></tr><tr><td>13</td><td></td></tr><tr><td>14</td><td></td></tr><tr><td>15</td><td>East and</td></tr><tr><td>16</td><td>North</td></tr><tr><td>17</td><td>regions</td></tr></table> The text is now completely visible and appears in the bottom three lines of the merged cell.
Click [↰]	To undo the wrapped text.
3 In the Alignment group, click [✏▾]	To display the Orientation menu.
Choose **Rotate Text Up**	To rotate the text 90 degrees.
Click [≡]	(The Middle Align button is in the Alignment group.) To center the text vertically in the cell.
Click [≡]	(The Center button is in the Alignment group.) To center the text horizontally in the cell.
4 Click [**B**]	(The Bold button is in the Font group.) To make the text bold. The text in A5 is now displayed vertically, centered in the merged cell, and bold, as shown in Exhibit 2-9.
5 Update the workbook	

Splitting merged cells

Explanation

After you have merged a range of cells, you might need to split them. To do so, select the merged cell, click the arrow on the Merge & Center button in the Alignment group, and choose Unmerge Cells.

Do it!

E-3:   Splitting cells

Here's how	Here's why
1 Click the **Split cells** sheet	This worksheet contains the bonus sales report for four salespeople. The table title is merged and centered across the five columns containing the sales report. You'll add the bonus sales details for a fifth salesperson, split the merged cells containing the table title, and then merge cells again so that the title extends over all six columns.
2 In F4, enter **Tina Ralls**	To enter the name of the fifth salesperson.
3 In F5:F8, enter data as shown	$4,600 $5,200 $4,900 $1,550
4 Apply and remove borders for the new column of data so that it matches the other columns, as shown	(table shown) George / Henry Jones / Tina Ralls $3,958 $8,284 $4,600 $5,858 $4,555 $5,200 $4,879 $3,432 $4,900 $5,550 $7,660 $1,550
5 Select A3	The range A3:E3 is selected because the cells in this range are merged.
Click the arrow on the Merge & Center button and choose **Unmerge Cells**	Merge & Center Merge Across Merge Cells Unmerge Cells To split the cells in the range A3:E3.
6 Select A3:F3	You'll merge cells and center the table title across the new range.
Click Merge & Center	The cells are merged, and the table title is centered across all six columns.
7 Update the workbook	

Transposing data

Explanation

There may be times when you've entered data into rows that you should have put in columns, and vice versa. In Excel, you can quickly switch the placement of data in rows and columns by using the Transpose command.

The Transpose button is available in the Paste options. As shown in Exhibit 2-10, Paste Preview shows you how the pasted data will appear. To transpose rows and columns:

1   Select the range whose layout you want to switch.

2   Copy the selected range. You must copy the selection rather than cutting it; otherwise, the Paste Special options will not be available.

3   Select the cell where you want to paste the copy.

4   From the Paste menu, choose Transpose.

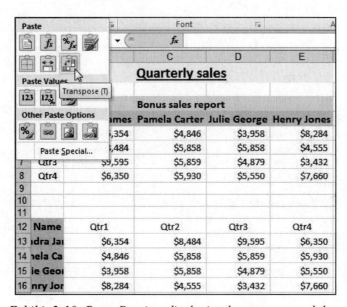

Exhibit 2-10: Paste Preview displaying how transposed data will appear.

Do it!

E-4: Transposing data during a paste

Here's how	Here's why
1 Click the **Transpose** sheet	You want the names to appear in the first column, rather than in the row they're in now.
2 Select A4:E8	
Right-click the selection and choose **Copy**	
3 Select A12	You'll paste the data here.
4 Display the **Paste** menu	

As you point to the options on the Paste menu, Paste Preview displays the results in the selected range.

Click	To transpose the row and column data.
Press ESC	To turn off the marquee around A4:E8.
5 Adjust the column widths	To make all the data visible.
Update the workbook	

Using Paste Special operations

Explanation

You can combine the values in one range with another by using the Paste Special mathematical operations, such as add, subtract, multiply, and divide. Paste Special operations can be performed only on ranges containing values, not on ranges with formulas.

To add values by using the Paste Special commands, use the following steps:

1 Select the range containing the data to be copied. Click Copy.

2 Select the range containing the data to be combined.

3 Right-click and choose Paste Special to open the Paste Special dialog box.

4 Under Operation, select Add.

5 Click OK. The values in the copied range will be added to the values in the destination range.

Do it!

E-5:   Using Paste Special to add values

Here's how	Here's why
1 On the Transpose sheet, in G4, enter **Highest sales**	You will add the sales figures from Kendra and Henry together.
2 Copy B5:B8	Kendra's quarterly sales figures.
Select G5	
Press CTRL + V	To paste Kendra's sales figures.
3 Copy E5:E8	Henry's quarterly sales figures.
Select G5	
4 Right-click and choose **Paste Special...**	To open the Paste Special dialog box.
Under Operation, select **Add**	Operation ○ None ◉ Add ○ Subtract
Click **OK**	Highest sales $14,638 $13,039 $13,027 $14,010
	Henry's and Kendra's sales figures are combined and the result is displayed in G5:G8.
5 In H4, enter **Divide**	
6 Copy B5:B8 and paste in H5	
Divide H5:H8 by C5:C8	Copy C5:C8. Select H5, choose Paste Special, select Divide, and click OK.
7 Format H5:H8 in the **General** number format	To better show the results.
8 Update the workbook	

Adding backgrounds to a worksheet

Explanation

You can add interest to a worksheet by adding a background color. Simply select the cells whose background color you want to change, and select a color in the Fill Color gallery.

In addition, you can insert a background graphic via the Background command. The Background command is available in the Page Setup group on the Page Layout tab. Unlike fill colors, however, background graphics do not print.

To add a background picture:

1 Click the Page Layout tab.
2 In the Page Setup group, click Background to open the Sheet Background dialog box.
3 Select the desired background picture.
4 Click Insert.

Do it!

E-6: Adding and deleting backgrounds

Here's how	Here's why
1 Click the **Background** sheet	
2 Select A1:F44	You'll add a background color to the cells in this range.
3 Click the **Home** tab	If necessary.
4 In the Font group, in the Fill Color gallery, select the indicated color	Theme Colors — Red, Accent 2, Lighter 80% All cells in the range now have the same background color.
5 Select A4:E23	You'll apply a different background color to this range so that it stands out.
In the Fill Color gallery, select a light color	To change the background color of the selected cells.
6 Click the **File** tab	
Choose **Print**	A print preview appears on the right. The background colors you applied will print.
7 Click the **Page Layout** tab	
Press ↶ twice	(The Undo button is on the Quick Access toolbar.) To delete the background you just applied. You'll use the Background command to insert a background.
Deselect the range	
8 In the Page Setup group, click **Background**	To open the Sheet Background dialog box.
Navigate to the current topic folder	Student Data folder Unit 2\Topic E.

9 Select **Background**

   Click **Insert**

Name	City	Emp #
Bill MacArthur	Ashford	17111
Jamie Morrison	Broad Brook	46721
Jim Adams	Canaan	42499
Rebecca Austin	Farmington	42617
Paul Anderson	North Franklin	46110
Cynthia Roberts	North Grosvenordale	13330
Rita Greg	North Windham	42220
Trevor Johnson	Pomfret	13631
Kevin Meyers	Pomfret Center	46551
Adam Long	Putnam	13668
Kendra James	Quinebaug	13235
Michael Lee	Rogers	42985
Sandra Lawrence	Scotland	46330
Mary Smith	South Willington	46910
James Overmire	South Windham	46344
Annie Philips	South Woodstock	13241

To insert the file as a picture in the worksheet's background. The background image can be seen through the data, making the data harder to read.

10 Add a light fill color to A4:E23

To set the range apart from the background image.

Preview the page

The worksheet background is not visible because pictures used as backgrounds do not print.

On the File tab, choose **Info**

To see the background and the shaded data in the file thumbnail.

11 Click the **Page Layout** tab

In the Page Setup group, click **Delete Background**

To delete the background picture. This won't affect the fill color in A4:E23.

Update the workbook

Adding watermarks

Explanation
A *watermark* is a printable graphic often added to documents to convey an attribute such as confidentiality or document ownership. Although Excel does not have a watermark feature, you can mimic a watermark by adding a picture to a section of a header or footer.

To mimic a watermark in a worksheet:

1   Click the Insert tab.

2   In the Text group, click Header & Footer. The Header & Footer Tools appear, adding a Design tab to the Ribbon.

3   Click in the header or footer section where you want to insert the watermark picture.

4   On the Design tab, in the Header and Footer Elements group, click Picture to open the Insert Picture dialog box.

5   Select a picture and click Insert.

Do it!

E-7:   Adding a watermark

The files for this activity are in Student Data folder **Unit 2\Topic E**.

Here's how	Here's why
1 Click the **Insert** tab	
In the Text group, click **Header & Footer**	To switch to Print Layout view, with the center header section selected. The Header & Footer Tools | Design tab is active.
Click the right header section	You'll insert a watermark picture here.
2 In the Header & Footer Elements group, click **Picture**	To open the Insert Picture dialog box.
Navigate to the current topic folder	Student Data folder Unit 2\Topic E.
3 Select **Confidential**	
Click **Insert**	To insert the picture.
4 Deselect the header section	Click any cell in the body of the worksheet. The new picture appears.
5 Update and close the workbook	

Unit summary: Advanced formatting

Topic A   In this topic, you applied **special number formats** to ZIP codes and phone numbers. You learned how to hide or display **zero values** in an entire worksheet and in a selected range. You also used custom formats to display data in specific formats.

Topic B   In this topic, you used functions to **format text**. You used UPPER, LOWER, and PROPER to change the case of text. You also used the SUBSTITUTE function to change one text character to another.

Topic C   In this topic, you learned about the built-in **styles** that Excel provides. Then you created and applied styles. You also modified styles.

Topic D   In this topic, you learned about the various **themes** that Excel provides. You then applied and modified themes.

Topic E   In this topic, you **merged cells**, changed the orientation of text in cells, and split merged cells. You also **transposed** and **added** data during paste operations. Finally, you added a **background**, and you inserted a picture to serve as a watermark.

Independent practice activity

In this activity, you'll create styles and apply them to other worksheets. You'll merge and center cells and use a function to format text. Then you'll apply a number format and add a watermark.

The files for this activity are in Student Data folder **Unit 2\Unit summary**.

1 Open Practice details and save it as **My practice details**. Verify that the Advanced formatting worksheet is active.

2 Create custom styles called **Company**, **Title1**, **Column heading**, and **Region** based on the current worksheet. Apply these styles to the Apply styles worksheet.

3 Merge and center the company name and the subtitle over the entire width of the data.

4 Use the PROPER function to capitalize the employee names as proper nouns.

5 Format the data in column D with a phone-number format. Compare your results to Exhibit 2-11.

6 Insert the Confidential watermark picture in the left footer section.

7 Update and close the workbook.

Outlander Spices			
Employee contract details			
Region	Name	Emp #	Phone number
East	Pamela Carter	17121	(907) 555-4024
East	Anna Morris	46321	(800) 555-1425
East	Rita Lawson	42449	(520) 555-0767
East	Sam Peters	42517	(635) 555-4581
North	Julie George	46160	(357) 555-2978
North	Diana Stone	13337	(526) 555-2440
South	Rob Dukes	42820	(246) 555-6657
South	Tammy Heiret	13691	(545) 555-5457
South	Sandy Stewart	46550	(632) 553-5235
South	Wendy Alto	13168	(677) 555-3760
South	Tina Ralls	13225	(327) 555-6636
West	Nikki Cleary	42983	(523) 555-6373
West	Davis Lee	46430	(527) 555-7872
West	David Ford	46950	(633) 555-4643
West	Julia Stockton	46343	(545) 555-6544
West	Sonia Mccormick	13641	(774) 555-4383

Exhibit 2-11: The Apply Styles worksheet after Step 5

Review questions

1 List the steps to apply a special number format.

2 True or false? When you apply special number formats to data, Excel changes both the cell's appearance and the cell's value.

3 What is one way to control the display of zero values in a cell?

4 What is a style?

5 Can you apply a watermark to an Excel spreadsheet?

Unit 3

Outlining and subtotals

Unit time: 45 minutes

Complete this unit, and you'll know how to:

A Create outlines to group and organize data, create custom views, and consolidate data from different worksheets.

B Summarize the data in a worksheet by creating automatic subtotals.

Topic A: Outlining and consolidating data

This topic covers the following Microsoft Office Specialist objectives for exam 77-882: Excel 2010.

#	Objective
4.3	**Manipulate workbook views**
	4.3.4 Create custom views

Outlining

Explanation

You can organize data in a worksheet by creating an outline, which groups data by levels. Each level contains a section of the data that you can expand or collapse. A worksheet outline can have up to eight levels of detail. You can also consolidate data from different worksheets to summarize the data.

To outline data:

1   Select the range of cells for which you want to create an outline.

2   Verify that the summary rows or columns you want to outline are located in the same position relative to the detailed data. For example, the summary columns might be located either to the right or to the left of the detailed data, but not in both positions.

3   Click the Data tab.

4   In the Outline group, click the Group button's arrow and choose Auto Outline.

After creating an outline, you can use the outline symbols to expand and collapse data, as shown in Exhibit 3-1 and Exhibit 3-2. You can also expand or collapse data by row or column level. You can click the lowest-level button to show all details, and click the highest-level button to hide all details. (The higher the number, the lower the outline level.) For example, if an outline has four levels, click 4 to show details of all four levels, and click 1 to hide all details.

Selecting a large range

When using a large worksheet, you might need to select a range that covers several screens. It can be difficult to select this range by dragging. Another way to select such a range is to click the first cell in the range, press and hold Shift, and click the last cell in the range.

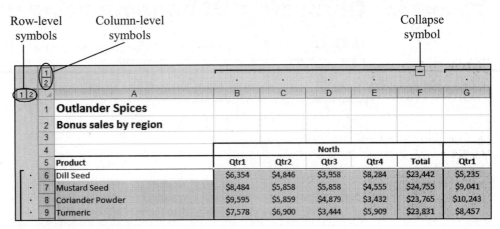

Exhibit 3-1: The expanded form

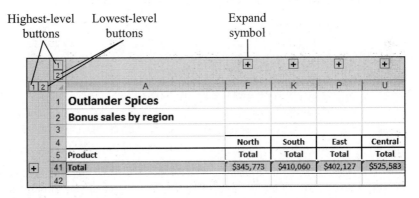

Exhibit 3-2: The collapsed form

Do it!

A-1: Creating an outline

The files for this activity are in Student Data folder **Unit 3\Topic A**.

Here's how	Here's why
1 Open Outline	The Quarterly sales worksheet contains more rows and columns than can typically be displayed when viewed at 100% magnification. You'll create an outline that displays only aggregate sales figures.
Save the workbook as **My outline**	In the current topic folder.
2 Select A6	To select the first cell in the range of data for which you'll create an outline.
Press and hold (SHIFT) and select Z41	To select the range A6:Z41.
Release (SHIFT)	
3 Click the **Data** tab	
In the Outline group, click **Group** as shown	To display the Group menu.
Choose **Auto Outline**	To outline the selected data. Various symbols appear above and to the left of the worksheet.
4 Click the collapse symbol above column F, as shown	(The collapse symbol resembles a minus sign.) To collapse the quarterly sales data for the North region and show only the total sales. There is now an expand symbol (+) above column F. The quarterly sales columns for the other regions are still visible.

5 Collapse the quarterly sales data for the other regions

		A	F
1		**Outlander Spices**	
2		**Bonus sales by region**	
3			
4			**North**
5		**Product**	**Total**
6		Dill Seed	$23,442
7		Mustard Seed	$24,755
8		Coriander Powder	$23,765

(Click the collapse symbols above columns K, P, U, and Z.) To display only the total sales data for the other regions. Expand symbols will appear above the five visible columns.

6 Click the expand symbol above column F

The quarterly sales data for the North region appears, and there is now a collapse symbol above column F.

7 Click the column-level symbol **2**, as shown

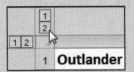

To expand the remaining collapsed column data.

8 Click the row-level symbol **1**

To collapse the row-level data. Detailed data for quarterly sales by product for each region disappears, and only the overall total of quarterly sales for each region is visible.

9 Click the row-level symbol **2**

To expand the row-level data. The worksheet displays the detailed data for the regions.

10 Collapse the column-level data

Click the column-level symbol 1.

Update the workbook

Creating custom views

Explanation

Views are sets of worksheet display and print settings that you can save. For example, in a sales worksheet, you can create a view in which the rows of data for all sales regions except for one are hidden. You can create multiple views for a worksheet and switch among them to change the display of the worksheet.

To create a view based on current display settings:

1   On the View tab, in the Workbook Views group, click Custom Views to open the Custom Views dialog box.

2   Click Add to open the Add View dialog box.

3   In the Name box, type a name for the view.

4   Click OK. Both the Add View and Custom Views dialog boxes close.

5   Click Custom Views again to see your new views, as shown in Exhibit 3-3.

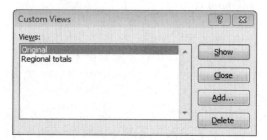

Exhibit 3-3: The Custom Views dialog box

Switching among custom views

To switch among views, open the Custom Views dialog box. From the Views list, select the view you want to display, and then click the Show button. You can also add the Custom Views command to the Quick Access toolbar to easily open that dialog box.

Do it!

A-2:   Creating custom views

Here's how	Here's why
1 Verify that only the product totals are visible	The column-level data has been collapsed.
2 Click the **View** tab	
3 In the Workbook Views group, click **Custom Views**	To open the Custom Views dialog box.
Click **Add**	To open the Add View dialog box.

4 In the Name box, enter
   Regional totals

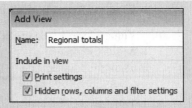

Click **OK**

Both the Add View and Custom Views dialog boxes close.

5 Click the **Data** tab

   In the Outline group, click
   Ungroup as shown

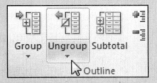

To display a menu.

Choose **Clear Outline**

To clear the outline and return the worksheet to its original state.

6 On the View tab, click
   Custom Views

To open the Custom Views dialog box. There is one custom view named "Regional totals." You'll create another view.

   Add a custom view named
   Original that shows the
   worksheet in its original state

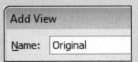

Click Add, enter Original, and click OK.

7 Open the Custom Views dialog
   box

(On the View tab, click Custom Views.) As shown in Exhibit 3-3, the Views list displays the two views you created. You can use this dialog box to switch between the views.

Select **Regional totals**

Click **Show**

To display the view showing only the regional totals for the product.

8 Display all quarterly product sales
   information

Open the Custom Views dialog box, select Original, and click Show.

9 Update and close the workbook

Consolidating data

Explanation

You can summarize data from different worksheets by using the data consolidation feature. Data can be consolidated by position or by category. Consolidate by *position* when the related data in the source worksheets is in the same location and order. Consolidate by *category* when data is not in the same location and order. Exhibit 3-4 shows an example of a worksheet with consolidated data.

		A	B	C	D	E	F
	1			**Outlander Spices**			
	2			**Bonus sales**			
	3						
	4			Qtr1	Qtr2	Qtr3	Qtr4
+	9		Anise Seeds	$2,725	$2,114	$2,467	$2,676
+	14		Asafoetida Powder	$2,674	$2,535	$2,553	$3,208
+	19		Basil Leaf (Whole)	$29,783	$28,751	$23,478	$33,117
+	24		Bay Leaf (Whole)	$1,773	$2,780	$2,620	$2,607
+	29		Caraway Seed (Whole)	$2,263	$3,084	$2,368	$2,112
+	34		Cardamom Seed (Whole)	$1,277	$2,199	$1,618	$2,619
+	39		Cardamom Seed (Ground)	$2,489	$2,760	$2,561	$2,804
+	44		Catnip Leaf	$3,447	$1,466	$1,870	$2,950
+	49		Celery Seed (Whole)	$24,232	$28,437	$23,697	$18,124
+	54		Chamomile Flowers	$1,770	$2,591	$2,323	$2,209

Exhibit 3-4: A worksheet with consolidated data

To consolidate data, click the Data tab. In the Data Tools group, click Consolidate to open the Consolidate dialog box, shown in Exhibit 3-5. The following table explains the options in this dialog box:

Option	Used to...
Function	Choose the aggregate function to consolidate data.
Reference	Specify the cell reference of the source data.
Browse	Navigate among workbooks.
Use labels in	Include row or column headings when you consolidate data by category. When you do not check this option, Excel does not copy category labels from the source area to the destination area.
Create links to source data	Reflect source-data changes in the consolidated data.

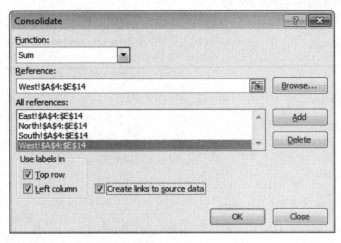

Exhibit 3-5: The Consolidate dialog box

Do it!

A-3: Using the Consolidate command

The files for this activity are in Student Data folder **Unit 3\Topic A**.

Here's how	Here's why
1 Open Consolidate	You'll consolidate the sales data for all products in the four regions.
Save the file as **My consolidate**	
2 Click the **Consolidating data** sheet	This is the worksheet where you'll put the consolidated data.
Select A4	
3 Click the **Data** tab	If necessary.
4 In the Data Tools group, click **Consolidate**	To open the Consolidate dialog box. In the Function list, Sum is selected by default.
Click ▦	(The Collapse Dialog button is in the Reference box.) To collapse the Consolidate dialog box. The title of the Consolidate dialog box changes to "Consolidate - Reference:" to indicate that the Reference box is active.
5 Click the **North** sheet	

6 Select A4:E14	Consolidate - Reference: North!$A$4:$E$14
	To specify the range that includes the product and quarter labels.
Click 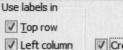	(The Expand Dialog button is in the Consolidate - Reference dialog box.) To expand the Consolidate dialog box.
Click **Add**	To add the range from the North worksheet to the All references list.
7 Click the **South** sheet	To create a reference to the South worksheet. The range A4:E14 is automatically selected. Excel takes the cell or range specified in the last reference as the default for each new reference. The value South!$A$4:$E$14 appears in the Reference box.
Click **Add**	To add the range from the South worksheet to the All references list.
8 Add the references from the East and West worksheets to the All references list	All references: East!$A$4:$E$14 North!$A$4:$E$14 South!$A$4:$E$14 West!$A$4:$E$14
	Click each worksheet, and click Add in the dialog box.
9 Under "Use labels in," check **Top row**	The Consolidating data worksheet becomes active. You'll consolidate data based on the labels in the top row. Excel copies the labels to the destination area when you consolidate data.
Under "Use labels in," check **Left column**	You'll consolidate data based on the labels in the left column.
Check **Create links to source data**	Use labels in ☑ Top row ☑ Left column ☑ Create links to source data
	To have Excel update the consolidated data automatically when changes are made in the source data. Compare your Consolidate dialog box to Exhibit 3-5.
Click **OK**	To close the Consolidate dialog box.

10	Deselect the cells	The worksheet shows the total product sales by quarter for the four regions. Outline symbols appear to the left of the worksheet. The worksheet should resemble Exhibit 3-4.

11 Click the row-level expand symbol next to row 9

4		Qtr1	Qtr2
5	My Consolidate	$734	$457
6	My Consolidate	$534	$423
7	My Consolidate	$833	$733
8	My Consolidate	$624	$501
9	Anise Seeds	$2,725	$2,114

To display the total sales of anise seeds by region. The total sales figure for each region is listed in the order you specified in the Consolidate dialog box. Excel uses the name of the workbook, "My Consolidate," as the label for each detail row.

Select C9

f_x =SUM(C5:C8)

The formula bar shows that the value in C9 is the result of adding C5:C8.

Select C5

f_x =East!$B$5

The formula bar shows the formula containing a link to the East worksheet.

12 Update and close the workbook

Topic B: Creating subtotals

Explanation

You can summarize data in a worksheet by calculating subtotals. You can automatically calculate subtotals and grand totals by using functions such as SUM and AVERAGE. You can also use multiple subtotals to summarize the data.

Subtotals in lists

If you want to create automatic subtotals, your list must contain column labels. Moreover, the list must be sorted so that the rows you want to subtotal are grouped together. For example, if you want subtotals for each region, then sort by region first to group the data. You can create subtotals for more than one type of calculation by using various summary functions, such as SUM, MAX, and MIN.

To create subtotals in a list:

1 Sort the list so that the rows you want to subtotal are grouped together.

2 Select any cell in the list and then click the Data tab.

3 In the Outline group, click Subtotal to open the Subtotal dialog box, shown in Exhibit 3-6.

4 From the "At each change in" list, select the column that contains the groups you want subtotaled.

5 From the "Use function" list, select the summary function you want to use.

6 In the "Add subtotal to" list, check the columns for which you want subtotals.

7 Click OK.

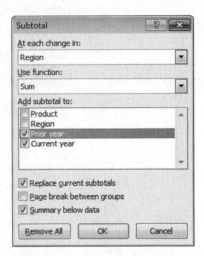

Exhibit 3-6: The Subtotal dialog box

Do it!

B-1: Creating subtotals in a list

The files for this activity are in Student Data folder **Unit 3\Topic B**.

Here's how	Here's why
1 Open Regional sales	
Save it as **My regional sales**	In the current topic folder.
Click the **Prior and current** sheet	This sheet contains sales totals for two years.
2 Select any cell in the range A4:D52	You'll calculate regional subtotals for the prior and current years' sales.
3 Click the **Data** tab	If necessary.
In the Outline group, click **Subtotal**	To open the Subtotal dialog box. The Sum function is selected by default. Excel automatically selects the sorted list in the worksheet.
4 From the "At each change in" list, select **Region**	To specify the column that contains the groups for which you want subtotals.
Under "Add subtotal to," check **Prior year**	As shown in Exhibit 3-6. The rightmost column, Current year, is checked by default. Prior year and Current year are the columns for which you'll create subtotals.
Click **OK**	To close the dialog box. The subtotals for each region appear, along with the grand total for all the regions. Notice that Excel outlines the data.
5 Click the second-level outline button	

To hide the detail.

Observe the worksheet

Region	Prior year	Current year
East Total	$447,458	$407,473
North Total	$422,339	$391,866
South Total	$593,807	$596,796
West Total	$605,386	$603,545
Grand Total	$2,068,990	$1,999,680

Only the regional subtotals and the grand totals appear.

Expand the sheet to display third-level details	Click the third-level outline button.
6 Update the workbook	

Multiple subtotal functions

Explanation

You can use more than one subtotal function to provide summary information. First, create a single set of subtotals based on one function. Then add the other functions one at a time. When you add a new function, be sure to clear the "Replace current subtotals" checkbox in the Subtotal dialog box.

Do it!

B-2: Using multiple subtotal functions

Here's how	Here's why
1 Verify that the **Prior and current** sheet is active	You'll add Max and Min subtotals to this list.
2 Select any cell in the list	(If necessary.) You'll use the MAX function to create subtotals for each region.
Open the Subtotal dialog box	(Click Subtotal in the Outline group.) The options you used earlier are selected.
3 From the Use function list, select **Max**	To display each region's maximum sales for the prior and current years.
Clear **Replace current subtotals**	Add subtotal to: ☐ Product ☐ Region ☑ Prior year ☑ Current year ☐ Replace current subtotals To retain the existing subtotals.
Click **OK**	The region's maximum sales and overall maximum sales for the Prior year and Current year columns appear.
4 Use the MIN function to add minimum subtotals for the Prior year and Current year columns	Use the Subtotal dialog box.
5 Update and close the workbook	

Unit summary: Outlining and subtotals

Topic A
In this topic, you created an **outline** to summarize data by levels. Next, you created **custom views** to save different sets of worksheet display and print settings. You also used the **Consolidate command** to summarize data from several ranges. You learned that you can consolidate by position or by category and that you can create links to the source data.

Topic B
In this topic, you created **subtotals** that summarize worksheet data. You used the Subtotal dialog box to create various summary formulas.

Independent practice activity

In this activity, you'll outline a sheet with a large amount of data to make it more manageable, and create subtotals.

The files for this activity are in Student Data folder **Unit 3\Unit summary**.

1 Open Practice outline. (Ensure that the Outlining worksheet is active.)

2 Save the workbook as **My practice outline**.

3 Create an automatic outline for the data in the Outlining worksheet.

4 Collapse columns and rows to display only summary information. Compare your worksheet to Exhibit 3-7.

5 In the Outlining worksheet, create a custom view named **Totals**.

6 Consolidate the data from the East and West worksheets, beginning in A4 in the Consolidate worksheet. (*Hint:* Use A4:E9 as the range in both sheets, use row and column labels, and link to the source data.)

7 Click the Subtotals worksheet.

8 Create subtotals for each product for the Prior year and Current year columns by using the SUM, AVERAGE, and MAX functions. Do not replace the current subtotals.

9 Update and close the workbook.

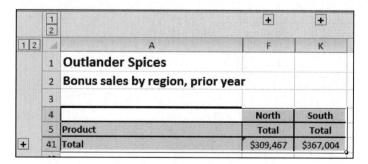

Exhibit 3-7: My practice outline after Step 4

Review questions

1 How does outlining help you work with large amounts of data?

2 When should you consolidate by position, and when should you consolidate by category?

3 How do you make the Consolidate command summarize data from multiple worksheets even if the row headings aren't in the same position in each sheet?

4 If you want to create automatic subtotals, what must your list contain?

5 How do you switch between views?

Unit 4

Cell and range names

Unit time: 55 minutes

Complete this unit, and you'll know how to:

A Use names to make your formulas easier to understand.

B Use the Name Manager and define 3-D names, which span multiple worksheets.

Topic A: Creating and using names

This topic covers the following Microsoft Office Specialist objectives for exam 77-882: Excel 2010.

#	Objective
1.1	**Navigate through a worksheet**
	1.1.2 Use the Name box
5.5	**Apply named ranges in formulas**
	5.5.1 Define ranges in formulas
	5.5.2 Edit ranges in formulas
5.6	**Apply cell ranges in formulas**
	5.6.2 Define a cell range

Defining names for cells or ranges

Explanation

A *name* is a meaningful description that you assign to a cell or range. After a name has been assigned, you can use it in formulas in place of cell references, making your formulas easier to understand. For example, in the formula =SUM(Qtr1), Qtr1 is the name assigned to the range of cells containing Quarter 1 data.

Names must begin with a letter or an underscore, cannot include spaces, and cannot match a cell address. For example, Q_1 is a valid name, but Q 1 is not (because of the space), and Q1 is not (because it's a cell address).

To define a name:

1 Select the cell or range that you want to name.

2 Enter the name in the Name box at the left edge of the formula bar.

You can select a named range in the worksheet by choosing it from the Name list. To display this list, click the arrow to the right of the Name box.

Do it!

A-1: Naming and selecting ranges

The files for this activity are in Student Data folder **Unit 4\Topic A**.

Here's how	Here's why
1 Open Teams	You'll define names to represent ranges in this workbook. You'll also use these names in formulas.
2 Save the workbook as **My teams**	In the current topic folder.
Verify that the Team sales worksheet is active	
3 Select A5:D5	You'll name this range Bloom.
Edit the Name box to read **Bloom**	Bloom ▾ 𝑓𝑥 The Name box is located at the left edge of the formula bar.
Press (↵ ENTER)	
4 Select A14:D14	
Name the range **Hanson**	Click in the Name box, type Hanson, and press Enter.
Name A23:D23 **Smith**	
5 From the Name list, select **Bloom**, as shown	Smith ▾ Bloom Hanson Smith (Display the Name list by clicking the arrow to the right of the Name box.) Cells A5:D5, the cells represented by the name Bloom, are selected.
6 Update the workbook	

Using a named range as a reference in a formula

Explanation

One of the primary reasons to name a range is so you can use the name in a formula to make it easier to understand. For example, =SUM (Qtr1_Sales) is more readily identifiable than =SUM (B3:B15). After a cell or range has been named, you can substitute the name for the cell address or range address in a formula.

To use a name in a formula, you can do either of the following:

- In the Defined Names group on the Formulas tab, click Use in Formula; then select the name you want to use in the formula.

- Begin typing the name in the formula; then select an item from the AutoComplete list that appears. The defined-name icon appears to the left of named ranges. You can use arrow keys to select the item and then press Tab to enter it in the formula.

Do it! **A-2: Using names in formulas**

Here's how	Here's why
1 Click the **Formulas** tab	
Select B31	You'll use the name Bloom instead of the range address to add the quarterly sales values for the Bloom team.
2 Type **=SUM(**	To begin the SUM function. You'll select the named range from a list.
3 In the Defined Names group, click **Use in Formula**	
	To display a list of named cells and ranges.
Select **Bloom**	To add the name to the formula you began.
4 Press (↵ ENTER)	To complete the formula.
5 Select B31	
Observe the formula	The formula =SUM(Bloom) is easier to understand than one that contains a range address.
6 Select B32	(If necessary.) You'll use AutoComplete to enter the name.
Type **=SUM(H**	A list of possible names and functions appears.
In the list, double-click **Hanson**	To add it to the formula.
Press (↵ ENTER)	To complete the formula.
7 In B33, enter a formula that sums the bonus sales of the Smith team	Use any method you like.
8 Update the workbook	

The Create from Selection command

Explanation

It can be tedious to create named ranges by manually entering each name. Instead, you can use column and row labels as names for the cells they represent. Here's how:

1   Select the range or ranges you want to name, including the row or column labels. (The cells containing the row or column labels won't be included in the named range. They are selected to provide the appropriate labels.)

2   In the Defined Names group on the Formulas tab, click Create from Selection to open the Create Names from Selection dialog box, shown in Exhibit 4-1.

3   Specify the locations of the labels in the selected range.

4   Click OK.

Exhibit 4-1: The Create Names from Selection dialog box

Do it!   **A-3:   Using the Create from Selection command**

Here's how	Here's why
1 Click the **East** sheet	
Select A5:E9	By using the labels in the range A5:A9, you'll name the respective rows in the range B5:E9. For example, B5:E5 will use the label "Anise Seeds."
2 In the Defined Names group, click **Create from Selection**	To open the Create Names from Selection dialog box, shown in Exhibit 4-1. "Left column" is checked because the selected range contains labels in the left column.
Click **OK**	To close the dialog box, creating a name for each row in the range B5:E9.
3 Select B5:E5	Anise_Seeds ▼
	The name of the selected range appears as Anise_Seeds. Excel adds an underscore to the label to make the name conform to the naming requirements.
4 Observe the names of the ranges B6:E6, B7:E7, B8:E8, and B9:E9	Select a range and observe the Name box.
5 Click the **West** sheet	You'll name ranges in this sheet.
6 Name cells B4:F9 by using the top row labels	(Select B4:F9 and click Create from Selection; then click OK.) If you don't select the top row labels (B4:F4), names will not be created.
Verify that names have been created	(Click the Name box's arrow.) You should see the names Qtr_1, Qtr_2, Qtr_3, Qtr_4, and Total in the list.
7 Update the workbook	

The Apply Names command

Explanation

You might work with spreadsheets in which formulas have already been entered with cell references rather than with named ranges. If you want to replace those references in formulas, you can use the Apply Names command.

Apply Names is also useful—particularly for copying formulas—if you enter formulas after creating names. If you AutoFill or copy and paste a formula that uses a named range, Excel treats that name as an absolute reference (as it would a cell reference like $B$10). For example, when you copy =SUM(Q1_sales) to the column to its right, the formula will still be =SUM(Q1_sales), not = SUM(Q2_sales) as you might expect.

In this instance, you can create the formula without using the named range, and then use the Apply Names command to replace the cell reference in each autofilled cell with its equivalent name.

To apply names:

1   Select cells that contain formulas with cell references that you want to replace with names.

2   In the Defined Names group on the Formulas tab, click the Define Name button's arrow and choose Apply Names. The Apply Names dialog box, shown in Exhibit 4-2, opens.

3   In the Apply names list, select the names you want to apply. You need only click to add to the selection (unlike with many lists, in which you need to Shift+click or Ctrl+click).

4   Click OK.

Exhibit 4-2: The Apply Names dialog box

Do it!

A-4: Applying names to existing formulas

Here's how	Here's why
1 Select B10	
2 Observe the formula bar	f_x =SUM(B5:B9) Because this formula was created before you defined names for the Qtr columns, the argument in the formula is the range B5:B9, not Qtr_1.
Observe the formulas for C10, D10, E10, and F10	These SUM formulas also use cell references, not names. You'll apply the names you created to these formulas.
Select B10:F10	
3 Click the arrow on the Define Name button and choose **Apply Names...**	(In the Defined Names group.) To open the Apply Names dialog box, shown in Exhibit 4-2.
Verify that the Qtr and Total names are selected, as shown	Apply names: Bay_Leaf Bloom Caraway_Seed Cinnamon Hanson Outlander_Spices Qtr_1 Qtr_2 Qtr_3 Qtr_4 Smith Total
Click **OK**	To close the dialog box and apply these names.
4 Select B10	f_x =SUM(Qtr_1) In the formula bar, the range has been replaced by the name Qtr_1.
Observe the formulas for C10, D10, E10, and F10	The SUM formulas use names instead of cell references. Another reason to apply names is that AutoFill will not work as you'd likely intend if you use it when starting with a named range.
5 Click the **East** sheet	You'll total the Anise_Seeds range.

6   Select F5

    In the Function Library group, click the AutoSum icon

                                       (Click the icon, not the arrow.) The AutoSum button automatically inserts the name rather than the range address.

    Press ⏎ ENTER   The formula refers to the name Anise_Seeds.

7   Select F5; then drag its AutoFill handle down to fill F6:F9   The value in F5 repeats because each formula sums the Anise_Seeds range.

    On the Quick Access toolbar, click ⟲ twice   To delete the values in each of the Total column cells.

8   Select B5:F9

    Click the AutoSum icon   To automatically sum the quarterly sales.

    Select F5 and observe the formula   When applied to a range, the AutoSum button inserts cell references, not names, in each cell.

9   Click the **Formulas** tab

    Select F5:F9   You'll replace the cell references with names.

10   Click the arrow on the Define Name button and choose **Apply Names...**   To open the Apply Names dialog box.

     Select names as shown

                                       Click each name to select it.

     Click **OK**   To close the dialog box and apply the names.

     Check each formula in F5:F9   The named ranges appear instead of the cell references.

11   Update and close the workbook

Topic B: Managing names

This topic covers the following Microsoft Office Specialist objectives for exam 77-882: Excel 2010.

#	Objective
5.5	**Apply named ranges in formulas**
	5.5.2 Edit ranges in formulas

The Name Manager

Explanation

When you create names in a workbook with multiple worksheets, you might need to manage the names to avoid reference problems. For example, if you create the same name in multiple sheets, it might be unclear which range to go to or use in a formula. You can use the Name Manager dialog box and 3-D names to handle named ranges in multiple sheets.

When you've created several names in a workbook, you might find the Name Manager dialog box, shown in Exhibit 4-3, useful for viewing and editing their properties. You can also use it to define new names and to delete multiple names quickly. To open this dialog box, click Name Manager in the Defined Names group on the Formulas tab.

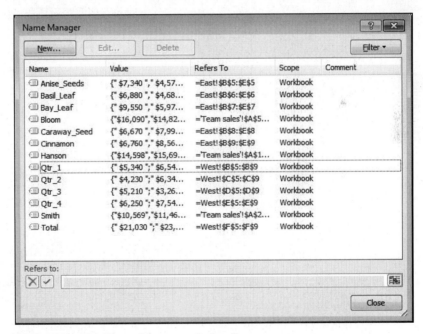

Exhibit 4-3: The Name Manager dialog box

Using the Name Manager to change and delete names

To use the Name Manager to modify a named range, select the name in the list and click Edit. The Edit Name dialog box opens, allowing you to edit the name itself, add comments, or change the cell references. When you are done making changes, click OK.

When you want to delete a named range, select the name in the Name Manager and click Delete. A message box will appear, asking you to confirm the deletion.

Do it!

B-1:   Modifying and deleting named ranges

The files for this activity are in Student Data folder **Unit 4\Topic B**.

Here's how	Here's why
1 Open Team sales	
Save the workbook as **My team sales**	
Click the **Team sales** sheet	You'll modify the defined names to include the Inventory costs column.
2 On the Formulas tab, in the Defined Names group, click **Name Manager**	To open the Name Manager dialog box. It contains a list of all names in the workbook, as well as their values and cell references.
3 In the Name list, select **Bloom**	When a name is selected in the list, the Edit and Delete buttons become available.
Click **Edit**	To open the Edit Name dialog box. You'll change the cell references in the name.
4 Click [icon]	Edit Name - Refers to: =' Team sales'!$A$5:$D$5 (The Collapse Dialog button is to the right of the Refers to box.) To collapse the dialog box and show only the cells that the name refers to. The range A5:D5 is selected in the worksheet.
Select A5:E5	To change the cell references to include the new column. The Edit Name - Refers to: box now includes the new range.
Click [icon]	To expand the dialog box.
5 Click **OK**	To close the Edit Name dialog box and apply the new range to the name.
Click **Close**	To close the Name Manager.
6 Scroll down to B31	The value has changed from $66,892 to $53,912.
7 Open the Name Manager	In the Defined Names group, click Name Manager.
In the Name list, select **Bloom**	

8	Click **Delete**	A message box appears, asking you to confirm the deletion.
	Click **OK**	To delete the name Bloom.
9	Click **Close**	To close the Name Manager. An error appears in B31 because the formula refers to a name that no longer exists.
	Update the workbook	

Using 3-D names

You can define names that refer to the same cell or range in multiple worksheets. These names are called *3-D names*. A 3-D name is typically useful in formulas that compile results from multiple sheets, such as one to total sales across multiple regions or time periods. Exhibit 4-4 shows a 3-D name that includes the cell F10 in all of the spreadsheets from the East sheet through the West sheet.

To create a 3-D name:

1 In the Name Manager dialog box, click New.

2 Delete the value in the Refers to box.

3 Click a sheet tab to establish the starting sheet in the range.

4 Hold Shift and click another sheet to define the ending sheet.

5 Click a cell to insert its address in the reference.

6 Click OK.

Exhibit 4-4: The New Name dialog box with a 3-D name defined

Do it!   **B-2:   Defining and applying 3-D names**

Here's how	Here's why
1 Open the Name Manager	
2 Click **New**	To open the New Name dialog box. You'll create a name for the combination of the Total cells in both regions.
In the Name box, enter **Regional_totals**	You'll define a 3-D name that refers to B10 across the worksheet range East:West.
In the Refers to box, delete the reference	If necessary.
3 Click 🗔	To collapse the New Name dialog box so it covers fewer cells in the workbook.
Click the **East** sheet	To specify the first worksheet to be referenced.
While holding (SHIFT), click the **West** sheet tab	To specify the last worksheet to be referenced in the range East:West.
Select F10	New Name - Refers to: ='East:West'!$F$10
	To specify the cell to be referenced across the specified worksheet range.
Click 🗔	(The Expand Dialog button is to the right of the Refers to box.) To expand the New Name dialog box.
4 Click **OK**	To add Regional_totals to the names list. This name will not appear in the Name box because it is a 3-D range, which refers to multiple worksheets.
Click **Close**	To close the Name Manager dialog box.
5 Click the **Total sales** sheet	(If necessary.) The formula that will refer to the Regional_totals range should go in F10.
6 Select F10	
7 Type **=SUM(Regional_totals)**	
8 Press (↵ ENTER)	The value of $241,400 is the sum of cells F10 in the East and West sheets.
9 Update and close the workbook	

Unit summary: Cell and range names

Topic A   In this topic, you defined **names** and selected **named ranges**. You used names in functions to make them more readable, and you created names from selections based on column and row labels. You also used the Apply Names command to replace the cell references in formulas with names.

Topic B   In this topic, you used the **Name Manager** to manage names. You edited a named range and deleted a name. You also created **3-D names**, which span multiple worksheets.

Independent practice activity

In this activity, you'll specify names for ranges within individual sheets and across multiple sheets.

The files for this activity are in Student Data folder **Unit 4\Unit summary**.

1 Open Practice names.

2 Save the workbook as **My practice names**.

3 On the Performance worksheet, define names to refer to the ranges B5:B20 and C5:C20. (*Hint:* Use the Create from Selection command, and include the column title in the selection.)

4 Apply the new names to the range B5:D21. Observe how names are used in the formulas in column D.

5 Define a 3-D name called **Regional_totals** that refers to F10 in the North and South sheets. Compare your Name Manager dialog box to Exhibit 4-5.

6 Use the name in a SUM formula in F10 in the Total sales sheet.

7 Delete the name **Regional_totals**.

8 Update and close the workbook.

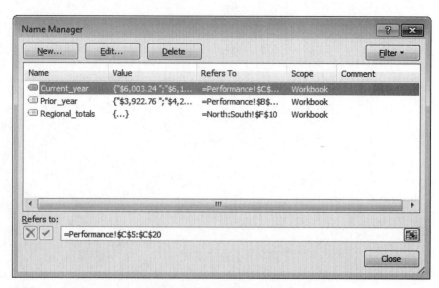

Exhibit 4-5: The Name Manager dialog box after Step 5

Review questions

1 What is a name in Excel?

2 True or false? Names must begin with a letter or an underscore and can include spaces.

3 What command can you use to create several names simultaneously?

4 What is the advantage of using a named cell or range in a formula?

5 True or false? By default, a cell name can be referenced from any sheet in a workbook.

6 How can you create a 3-D name to span multiple worksheets?

Unit 5

Tables

Unit time: 55 minutes

Complete this unit, and you'll know how to:

A Organize data logically, sort it by the contents of its columns, and filter it to show only those rows that meet certain criteria.

B Use the Custom AutoFilter and Advanced Filter dialog boxes to filter data based on complex criteria.

C Create and format tables, and use structured references to include table column names in formulas.

Topic A: Sorting and filtering data

This topic covers the following Microsoft Office Specialist objectives for exam 77-882: Excel 2010.

#	Objective
8.1	**Filter data**
	8.1.4 Filter lists using AutoFilter
8.2	**Sort data**
	8.2.1 Use sort options
	8.2.1.1 Values
	8.2.1.2 Font color
	8.2.1.3 Cell color

The structure of organized data

Explanation

You can organize your worksheet data in a concise and logical format by using rows containing related data.

Organized data is made up of records, fields, and field names. *Records* are simply rows of data in a range. *Fields* are the columns of data in a range. *Field names* are the column headings, which appear in the first row. Exhibit 5-1 shows Excel data organized in rows and columns of related information.

	A	B	C	D	E	F	
1	**Employee information**						
2							
3	**Name**	**Emp code**	**Empl #**	**Region**	**Department**	**Earning ($)**	Field name
4	Diana Stone	30	16-281	East	Marketing	60000	
5	Jesse Bennet	23	43-701	South	Sales	250500	
6	Rita Greg	9	42-800	East	Sales	380050	
7	Adam Long	18	16-586	North	Administration	90000	Record
8	Anna Morris	26	16-162	West	Accounts	150000	
9	Annie Philips	6	16-429	West	Human resources	60000	
10	David Ford	38	43-786	North	Customer support	150200	
11	Davis Lee	37	43-320	East	Accounts	73500	Field
12	James Overmire	4	43-190	South	Marketing	105000	
13	Jamie Morrison	19	42-901	East	Human resources	62000	
14	Julia Stockton	39	43-283	West	Customer support	96600	
15	Kevin Meyers	17	16-656	West	Accounts	84000	

Exhibit 5-1: The structure of organized data

Do it!

A-1:   Examining the structure of data

The files for this activity are in Student Data folder **Unit 5\Topic A**.

Here's how	Here's why
1 Open Employee list	You'll examine the structure of the Employee information.
Save the workbook as **My employee list**	In the current topic folder.
2 Observe A3:F3	The column headings in this range are the field names for this data.
3 Observe A5:F5	This row represents one record. In this range, each record contains all of the related information for an individual employee.
4 Observe A4:F43	Each cell represents a field value for a specific record.

Sorting data

Explanation

Sorting refers to organizing the data in ascending or descending order by the contents of one or more columns. *Filtering* refers to displaying only the information that meets specific criteria.

To sort data, select any cell in the column by which you want to sort. Click the Data tab. In the Sort & Filter group, click the Sort Ascending button or the Sort Descending button. This will sort the entire range, including all records, not just the column containing the selected cell.

You can also sort a range of data based on content in two or more columns. For example, you can sort employee information by region and department, as shown in Exhibit 5-2. In this case, all employees in a single region are grouped together and then sorted by department.

	A	B	C	D	E	F
1	**Employee information**					
2						
3	**Name**	**Emp code**	**Empl #**	**Region**	**Department**	**Earning ($)**
4	Melissa James	7	16-129	East	Accounts	87000
5	Davis Lee	37	43-320	East	Accounts	73500
6	Wendy Alto	34	43-730	East	Administration	105000
7	Sonia McCormick	40	16-192	East	Administration	78000
8	Roger Williams	5	43-763	East	Customer support	90000
9	Malcolm Pingault	1	16-891	East	Human resources	72000
10	Paul Anderson	11	43-133	East	Human resources	180000
11	Jamie Morrison	19	42-901	East	Human resources	62000
12	Diana Stone	30	16-281	East	Marketing	60000
13	Sandy Stewart	33	43-129	East	Marketing	65000
14	Rita Greg	9	42-800	East	Sales	380050
15	Kendra James	16	16-111	East	Sales	144000
16	Sandra Lawrence	15	43-487	North	Accounts	100000

Exhibit 5-2: The employee data sorted by Region and Department

To sort data based on two or more columns:

1   Select any cell in the range.

2   Click the Data tab.

3   In the Sort & Filter group, click Sort to open the Sort dialog box, shown in Exhibit 5-3.

4   From the Sort by list, select the heading of the column by which you want to sort. Then select a sorting order. All records will be sorted first based on the column and the sorting order you selected.

5   Click Add Level to add another sort level. From the Then by list, select the next column by which you want to sort, and select the sort order.

6   Click OK.

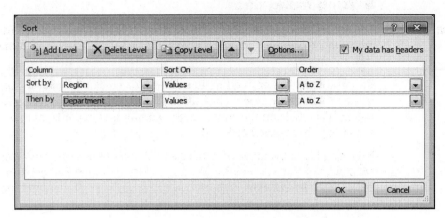

Exhibit 5-3: The Sort dialog box, with a second sort level added

Do it! **A-2: Sorting data**

Here's how	Here's why
1 Select B4	You'll sort the rows of employee information by the contents of this column, Emp code, in ascending order. You can select any cell in the column you want to sort by.
Click the **Data** tab	
2 In the Sort & Filter group, click ![A Z↓]	

Name	Emp code
Malcolm Pingault	1
Shannon Lee	2
Melinda McGregor	3
James Overmire	4
Roger Williams	5

(The Sort Smallest to Largest button.) The rows are now organized in ascending order by employee code.

Here's how	Here's why
3 Select any cell in the range	(If necessary.) You'll sort the data by multiple fields.
4 Click **Sort**	

![Sort button]

(The Sort button is in the Sort & Filter group.) To open the Sort dialog box.

Here's how	Here's why
Under Column, from the Sort by list, select **Region**	To specify that the data be sorted first by region.
Under Sort on, verify that **Values** is selected	To sort by the contents of the cells.
Under Order, select **A to Z**	(If necessary.) The range will be sorted by region in ascending (alphabetical) order.
5 Click **Add Level**	To add a second criterion to this sort.
6 Under Column, from the Then by list, select **Department**	When rows have the same value in the Region column, they will be sorted by department. The default order is Ascending, as shown in Exhibit 5-3.
Click **OK**	To display the sorted data in the worksheet. All employees in a region are now grouped together, beginning with the East region. For each region, the department names are sorted in ascending alphabetical order, as shown in Exhibit 5-2.
7 Update the workbook	

Filtering data

Explanation

You can *filter* a range of data when you want to display only those rows of information that meet specific criteria. To help you do this, Excel provides the AutoFilter feature.

Here's how it works:

1   Select any cell in the range.
2   Click the Data tab.
3   In the Sort & Filter group, click Filter to display the AutoFilter arrows next to the column headings.
4   From the AutoFilter menu for the column by which you want to filter, select one or more criteria, as shown in Exhibit 5-4.
5   Click OK.

To clear the filter and show the entire range of data, click Filter again.

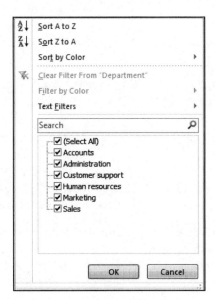

Exhibit 5-4: The AutoFilter menu

Do it!

A-3:   Filtering data by using AutoFilter

Here's how	Here's why
1 Select any cell in the range	
2 Click the **Data** tab	If necessary.
3 Click **Filter**	In the Sort & Filter group.
Observe the column headings	An AutoFilter arrow appears to the right of each column heading.

Name	▼	Emp co(	▼	Empl #	▼	Regior	▼	Department	▼

4 Click the AutoFilter arrow next to Department	To display a menu of sorting and filtering criteria, as shown in Exhibit 5-4.
5 Clear **Select All**	To clear the department selections.
Check **Accounts**	To display only the records of employees in the Accounts department. All other records will be hidden.
Click **OK**	To filter the data.
6 Observe the AutoFilter button	

Regior	▼	Department	▼	Earning	▼

	Notice the funnel icon. The AutoFilter button indicates that a filter has been applied to the Department column.
7 Click the AutoFilter arrow next to Region, and select only **West**	To display only the records of those employees in the Accounts department who work in the West region.
8 Click the AutoFilter arrow next to Department and choose **Clear Filter from "Department"**	The data is no longer filtered by department.
Clear the Region filter	(Click the AutoFilter arrow and choose Clear Filter from "Region.") The data is no longer filtered by region.
9 Update the workbook	

Using other criteria to sort and filter data

Explanation   You can use a variety of criteria to sort and filter data. For example, you can use a cell color or font color as your sorting or filtering criterion. You can also select a cell and sort your data based on that cell's attributes, such as its formatting or its value.

To sort and filter data based on cell color or font color, click the arrow next to the column heading that contains the values you want to sort or filter. From the menu, choose Sort by Color or Filter by Color, and select the fill or font color by which you want to sort or filter.

To sort and filter based on a cell's attributes, right-click the selected cell. From the shortcut menu, choose the option you want to sort or filter by.

Do it!   ### A-4:   Using cell color and attributes to sort and filter data

Here's how	Here's why
1 Observe the Earning column	The values in this column have been conditionally formatted to highlight the top 10 earning values in light red, and the bottom 10 values in light green.
Display the sort-and-filter menu for the Earning column	(Click the AutoFilter arrow on the column heading.) You'll sort the column based on one of the conditional formats.
2 Choose **Sort by Color**	To display a submenu.
Click as shown	
	To sort by the indicated fill color. The data is sorted with the bottom 10 earning values now at the top.
3 Select F21	You'll filter the data by the value in this cell.
Right-click the cell	To display a shortcut menu.
4 Choose **Filter**, **Filter by Selected Cell's Value**	To find all of the column values that match the value in the selected cell. Two records appear.
5 Clear the filter	Click Filter.
Update and close the workbook	

Topic B: Advanced filtering

This topic covers the following Microsoft Office Specialist objectives for exam 77-882: Excel 2010.

#	Objective
8.1	**Filter data**
	8.1.1 Define a filter
	8.1.2 Apply a filter
	8.1.3 Remove a filter
	8.1.4 Filter lists using AutoFilter

Custom AutoFilters

Explanation

You can filter data based on two or more criteria by using Excel's advanced filtering features. For example, you can display the records of all employees whose department is either Marketing or Sales. Excel provides the Custom AutoFilter and Advanced Filter tools for specifying multiple filtering criteria.

Use the Custom AutoFilter dialog box to specify multiple criteria for the same column heading, as shown in Exhibit 5-5.

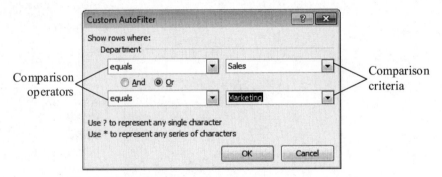

Exhibit 5-5: The Custom AutoFilter dialog box

In Exhibit 5-5, Department is the column on which the data will be filtered. The first criterion states that the department must be Sales; the second criterion states that the department must be Marketing. The two criteria are joined by the Or operator, meaning that rows will be included in the filtered data if they meet *either* criterion. When you use the And operator, the rows must meet *both* criteria. The criteria shown in Exhibit 5-5 would yield all employees who work in either the Sales or Marketing departments.

To filter data by using the Custom AutoFilter dialog box:

1 Turn on AutoFilter.

2 Display the drop-down menu for the column for which you want to create criteria. Then choose Text Filters, Custom Filter to open the Custom AutoFilter dialog box.

3 Select the first comparison operator and its associated criterion.

4 Select And or Or. By selecting And, you'll decrease the number of rows that meet the criteria. By selecting Or, you'll increase the number of matching rows.

5 Select the second comparison operator and its associated criterion.

6 Click OK.

Do it!

B-1: Using Custom AutoFilter criteria

The files for this activity are in Student Data folder **Unit 5\Topic B**.

Here's how	Here's why
1 Open Employees	
Save the workbook as **My employees**	In the current topic folder.
2 Click **Filter**	 ▼ Filter To enable filtering.
Click the AutoFilter arrow next to Department	To display the sorting and filtering criteria. You'll display the records of those employees who belong to either the Sales department or the Marketing department.
3 Choose **Text Filters**, **Custom Filter...**	To open the Custom AutoFilter dialog box. In the upper-left list, the first comparison operator, equals, is selected.
From the upper-right list, select **Sales**	To specify the first comparison criterion.
Show rows where: Department equals ▼ Sales	
Select **Or**	This tells Excel to display all records that match either of the two comparison criteria.
4 From the lower-left list, select **equals**	To specify the second comparison operator.
From the lower-right list, select **Marketing**	To specify the second comparison criterion. The Custom AutoFilter dialog box now resembles Exhibit 5-5.
Click **OK**	The worksheet displays 14 records of employees who work in either the Sales department or the Marketing department.
5 In the Sort & Filter group, click **Clear**	The data is no longer filtered by these two criteria. AutoFilter remains active.

Creating a criteria range

Explanation

You can filter records based on two or more column headings by using multiple criteria. For example, you can filter data to display the records of all East region employees whose salaries are greater than $100,000, and all West region employees whose salaries are greater than or equal to $80,000. A criteria range filters data based on complex criteria.

A *criteria range* is a cell range containing a set of search conditions. It consists of one row of criteria labels and at least one row that defines the search conditions. Each criterion label must be the name of a column for which you want to specify a criterion. The Advanced Filter dialog box filters a range of data according to a criteria range.

The following table lists the comparison operators that can be used in a criteria range:

Operator	Meaning
=	Equal to
>	Greater than
<	Less than
>=	Greater than or equal to
<=	Less than or equal to
<>	Not equal to

To create a criteria range by using the Advanced Filter dialog box:

1 Enter at least one criterion label in a cell that is *not* adjacent to the range containing the data. The criterion label must be exactly the same as the column heading in the data range.

2 Below the cell that contains the criterion label, enter a comparison criterion.

3 Click the Data tab.

4 In the Sort & Filter group, click Advanced to open the Advanced Filter dialog box.

5 In the List range box, enter the range you want to filter. The range must include the associated column headings.

6 In the Criteria range box, enter the range that contains your criteria.

7 Click OK.

▲	A	B	C	D	E	F
3	Name	Emp code	Empl #	Region	Department	Earning ($)
15	Wendy Alto	34	43-730	East	Administration	105000
18	Paul Anderson	11	43-133	East	Human resources	180000
19	Rita Greg	9	42-800	East	Sales	380050
20	Kendra James	16	16-111	East	Sales	144000
35	Kevin Meyers	17	16-656	West	Accounts	84000
36	Maureen O'Connor	20	42-212	West	Accounts	120000
37	Pamela Carter	25	43-517	West	Accounts	84000
38	Anna Morris	26	16-162	West	Accounts	150000
39	Rita Lawson	27	42-521	West	Accounts	106000
40	Tina Ralls	35	16-497	West	Administration	124000
41	Julia Stockton	39	43-283	West	Customer support	96600
42	James Owens	24	16-871	West	Marketing	92000
43	Cynthia Roberts	13	43-129	West	Sales	136000

Exhibit 5-6: The data with an advanced filter consisting of two criteria

Do it!

B-2: Using the Advanced Filter dialog box

Here's how	Here's why
1 In H3, enter **Region**	To specify the first criterion label. Ensure that it exactly matches the column heading in the data range. Copying and pasting the column headings is a good way to ensure that the labels are identical to those in the data range.
In I3, enter **Earning ($)**	To specify the second criterion label. Be sure to include the space between *Earning* and *($)*. (You can copy and paste the heading from F3.)
2 In H4, enter **East**	To specify East as the first comparison criterion.
In I4, enter **>100000**	To complete the first row of criteria. These criteria will display only those values in the East region with earnings greater than $100,000.
3 In H5, enter **West**	To specify West as the criterion.
In I5, enter **>=80000**	The second row of the criteria range will display values in the West region with earnings greater than or equal to $80,000. Adding rows to a criteria range amounts to using an Or operator, so rows will be included if they meet either of these conditions.
4 Select any cell in the original data range	(In the range A4:F43.) You'll enter the entire data range automatically when you choose the Advanced Filter command.
In the Sort & Filter group, click **Advanced**	To open the Advanced Filter dialog box. "Filter the list, in-place" is selected by default. This means that the filtered data will be displayed in the same worksheet. The entire data range appears selected in the worksheet.

5   Collapse the Criteria range box

(Click the Collapse Dialog button.) The Advanced Filter - Criteria range: dialog box appears.

Select H3:I5

Region	Earning ($)
East	>100000
West	>=80000

To enter the criteria range.

6   Expand the Criteria range box

The Advanced Filter dialog box expands.

Click **OK**

As shown in Exhibit 5-6, the records of the four employees in the East region whose salaries are greater than $100,000 are displayed, as well as the records of the nine employees in the West region whose salaries are greater than or equal to $80,000.

7   Display the unfiltered data

Click Clear in the Sort & Filter group.

8   Update the workbook

Copying filtered results to another location

Explanation

In the examples you've seen so far, rows are filtered out of the data so that all you can see are the remaining rows. You can also choose to keep the original data intact and place a copy of the filtered data somewhere else in the same worksheet or in another worksheet in the workbook. To do so, select the "Copy to another location" option in the Advanced Filter dialog box, and then specify a starting cell for the copied data, as shown in Exhibit 5-7.

Exhibit 5-7: Using the Advanced Filter dialog box to copy the filtered data to another location

Do it!

B-3: Copying filtered results to another range

Here's how	Here's why
1 Select a cell in the Name column	If necessary.
2 Open the Advanced Filter dialog box	(Click Advanced in the Sort & Filter group.) The list and criteria ranges that were previously entered in the dialog box are still there.
3 Select **Copy to another location**	The Copy to box is enabled.
Beside the Copy to box, click [image]	To open the Advanced Filter - Copy to: dialog box.
Select H10	This cell will be the starting point for the filtered result.
4 Expand the dialog box	So it looks like Exhibit 5-7.
Click **OK**	The worksheet displays the filtered data in the specified location.
5 Update and close the workbook	

Topic C: Working with tables

This topic covers the following Microsoft Office Specialist objectives for exam 77-882: Excel 2010.

#	Objective
5.5	**Apply named ranges in formulas**
	5.5.3 Rename a named range

Creating tables

Explanation

In Excel, you can convert your organized data into a *table*. When you define a range as a table, Excel automatically assigns it a name (such as "Table1"), applies a table format, and enables filtering. The rows and columns of a table can be changed independently of other worksheet rows and columns. Excel also changes the way you add data to the table and the way formulas refer to the cells in it.

You can convert a range of data to a table in three ways. Select a cell in the range, and then do any of the following:

- In the Styles group on the Home tab, select a table style from the Format as Table gallery.
- In the Tables group on the Insert tab, click Table.
- Press Ctrl+T.

Do it!

C-1: Creating a table

The files for this activity are in Student Data folder **Unit 5\Topic C**.

Here's how	Here's why
1 Open Product list	This workbook contains sheets with inventory and sales information.
Save the workbook as **My product list**	
2 Select any cell in the range A6:C19	You don't need to select the entire range; Excel will attempt to determine it automatically.
3 Click the **Insert** tab	
In the Tables group, click **Table**	To open the Create Table dialog box. The selected range is correct.
Click **OK**	To close the dialog box and create the table. By default, Excel applies a built-in style to the table.
4 Update the workbook	

Formatting tables

Explanation

After creating the table, you can control its formatting by choosing options on the Design tab (partially shown in Exhibit 5-8). This is a Table Tools contextual tab, which is displayed only when you're working with tables.

Exhibit 5-8: The Table Tools | Design tab

Settings in the Table Style Options group affect how Excel formats the rows and columns:

- The Header Row and Total Row options determine whether Excel formats the top and bottom rows. These options also affect how Excel references columns in formulas (as named ranges or as individual cells).

- The First Column and Last Column options determine whether Excel formats the leftmost and rightmost columns differently than the interior columns. Not all table styles apply first- and last-column formatting, so it might not matter whether this option is checked or not.

- The Banded Rows and Banded Columns options apply fill colors to alternating rows and alternating columns, which can make them easier to differentiate.

Choosing a table style from the Table Styles group changes the table's color scheme and borders. If you formatted the header and/or left column before creating the table, your original formatting will remain applied to those ranges, so only the body of the table will receive new formatting.

If you want to override all Table Style Options and return to the formatting you applied before creating the table, select the first table style, None. This table style doesn't initially appear in the Format as Table gallery; you can apply it only after the table has been created.

Do it!

C-2:   Formatting a table

Here's how	Here's why
1 Select a single cell in the table	To deselect the table so you can see its formatting without highlighted cells.
2 Verify that the Table Tools | Design tab is active	When you select a cell in a newly created table, Excel automatically activates the Table Tools | Design tab.
In the Table Style Options group, check **First Column**	To emphasize the first column according to the table style. On the Ribbon, the selected table style color changes and the text becomes bold.
3 In the Table Style Options group, uncheck **Header Row**	To hide the header row.
Uncheck **Banded Rows**	To turn off the alternating-row fill colors.
4 Turn on the header row	Check Header Row in the Table Style Options group.
Turn on banded columns	Check Banded Columns in the Table Style Options group.
5 Update the workbook	

Adding to a table

Explanation

When you enter data in a cell adjacent to a table, Excel automatically adds it to the table and formats the top row or left column cell to match. This behavior is an AutoCorrect option, which you can undo by clicking the AutoCorrect Options button and choosing Undo Table AutoExpansion.

To delete a row or column, you can right-click it and choose Delete, Table Columns or Table Rows. If you want to add or delete several rows and columns at once, you can click Resize Table in the Properties group on the Design tab and then specify a new range for the table.

Do it!

C-3:   Adding and deleting rows and columns

Here's how	Here's why
1 In D6, enter **Total value**	When you press Enter, Excel automatically formats the heading to match those to its left. An AutoCorrect Options button appears.
Click the AutoCorrect Options button as shown	![AutoCorrect Options menu showing: Undo Table AutoExpansion, Stop Automatically Expanding Tables, Control AutoCorrect Options...]
	To display options for the automatic action just taken.
Observe the options	You can undo the automatic expansion of the table, stop automatically expanding tables, or control all AutoCorrect options.
Press ⌐ESC⌐	To close the menu.
2 In A20, type **Cinnamon** and press ⌐TAB⌐	To create a new row. Excel automatically expands the table.
In B20, type **10** and press ⌐TAB⌐	
In C20, enter **400**	Next, you'll delete the row you just created.
3 Right-click any cell in the last row	To display a shortcut menu.
Choose **Delete**, **Table Rows**	To delete the new row.
4 Update the workbook	

Structured references

Explanation

After you create a table, you can use structured references in formulas that refer to data in the table. *Structured references* are references that use table names or column headings (or both) instead of cell or range addresses. When you use this feature, Excel automatically names table columns based on their headings (the values in the top row) and then uses those names in formulas, as shown in Exhibit 5-9. Structured references have a couple of advantages:

- Structured references can make formulas easier to understand. For example, "Unit price" is more meaningful than "A2," and "Qty in stock" is more meaningful than "B2."

- Structured references adjust automatically, so you don't need to rewrite formulas if you add rows or columns to, or delete rows or columns from, a table.

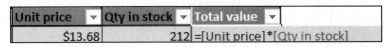

Exhibit 5-9: A formula using structured references

To use a structured reference when entering a formula, type "[" to begin a column reference. An AutoComplete list appears, showing the names of the table columns you can choose from. You can also type a formula with an A1-style cell reference; Excel won't replace it with a column name, so you can still create traditional formulas if you prefer.

When you complete the formula by pressing Enter, Excel's default AutoCorrect behavior fills (copies) the formula to all other cells in the column. If the formula refers to a column name, it will be the same in each cell. So, not only are formulas with structured references easier to read, but they are also less prone to errors. Because each cell can contain the exact same formula, it's more difficult to accidentally change one.

The Total row

A table can include one special row at the bottom that is designated as the Total row. Each of its cells can hold a function to summarize the data in the column above. However, instead of using SUM, AVERAGE, or a similar function, formulas in the Total row are created by default with the SUBTOTAL function. This function, depending on the arguments, can act like SUM, AVERAGE, or other functions.

The reason for this is that the SUBTOTAL function will display the correct value if you apply a filter to one or more columns. For example, if you apply a filter that hides all but two rows, as shown in Exhibit 5-10, the SUBTOTAL function in the Total row will sum just those values, not all values (including the hidden ones).

Unfiltered column   Filtered column

price	Qty in stock	Total value
$13.68	212	2900.16
$5.85	327	1912.95
$19.54	411	8030.94
$2.25	372	837
$12.23	406	4965.38
$51.29	483	24773.07
$31.75	557	17684.75
$31.78	491	15603.98
$53.12	433	23000.96
$24.37	312	7603.44
$54.74	101	5528.74
$42.01	234	9830.34
$9.87	329	3247.23
	4668	125918.94

rice	Qty in stock	Total value
$31.78	491	15603.98
$53.12	433	23000.96
$24.37	312	7603.44
$54.74	101	5528.74
$42.01	234	9830.34
$9.87	329	3247.23
	1900	64814.69

SUBTOTAL sums only visible values

SUBTOTAL sums all values

Exhibit 5-10: The SUBTOTAL function in the Total row operates only on visible cells

Excel creates a Total row automatically if you select a cell directly below the table and use the AutoSum button to create a formula, or if you check Total Row in the Table Style Options group on the Design tab.

Do it!

C-4: Using structured references

Here's how	Here's why
1 In D7, type **=[**	To begin creating a formula with structured references. An AutoComplete list appears, showing the table's column names.
In the list, double-click **Unit Price**	To add a column reference to the formula.
Type **]**	To complete the reference to the column name.
2 Type *****	To enter the multiplication operator.
Complete the formula as shown	f_x =[Unit price]*[Qty in stock]
	To calculate the unit price multiplied by quantity in stock. This formula is easier to read than one using cell or range addresses.

3	Press ⏎ ENTER	To complete the formula. When you use structured references, AutoCorrect adds a formula for each cell in the column.
	Observe the formula in D8	The formula in this cell, and in each cell in the column, is the same as the one you entered. All of these formulas refer to the column name, not to individual cells.
	Click the **Design** tab	(Under Table Tools on the Ribbon.) If necessary.
4	In the Table Style Options group, check **Total Row**	To add a Total row at the bottom of the table.
	Select D20 and observe the formula in it	The formula =SUBTOTAL(109,[Total value]) calculates the sum of the visible cells in the column.
		You'll experiment with other SUBTOTAL types.
5	From the drop-down list for D20, select **Average**, and then observe the formula	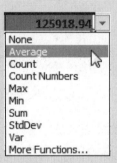
		The cell displays the average value. The first argument of the function changes from 109 (which represented Sum) to 101 (which represents Average).
	From the drop-down list for D20, select **Sum**	To reset the formula to calculate the sum.
6	Select C20	
	Click the **Formulas** tab	
	Click **AutoSum**	(Click the button, not its drop-down arrow.) Excel creates a SUBTOTAL function to sum the column.
		You'll now filter the table to test how the SUBTOTAL functions in the Total row work.
7	Click the AutoFilter arrow next to Product	To display the sorting and filtering criteria. You'll display only spices with names beginning with the letter C.

8	Choose **Text Filters**, **Begins With...**	To open the Custom AutoFilter dialog box. In the upper-left list, the first comparison operator, "begins with," is selected.
	In the upper-right box, enter **C**	Show rows where: Product [begins with ▼] [C]
	Click **OK**	To close the dialog box and filter the table so that only spice names beginning with C appear. The formulas in C20 and D20 sum only the visible values.
9	Select D20	
	Calculate the average of the displayed values	Click the arrow next to the cell and select Average.
10	Calculate the count of Product items in the displayed list	(Select A20, click the arrow next to the cell, and select Count.) There are six items.
	From the Product column's AutoFilter menu, choose **Clear Filter from "Product"**	To display all values. The count in A20 changes to 13.
11	Update the workbook	

Table names

Explanation

When you create a table, Excel automatically assigns it a name (Table1 for the first table in the workbook, Table2 for the second, etc.). If you create a formula in a cell outside the table, and the formula refers to columns inside the table, Excel will use structured referencing to insert the table name and column name in the formula, as shown in Exhibit 5-11. By default, formulas within the table don't use the table name, just as most formulas don't include the worksheet name unless it's necessary.

fx   =AVERAGE(Table1[Unit price])

Exhibit 5-11: A formula that refers to the Unit price column in the Table1 table

You can edit the table's name in the Properties group on the Table Tools | Design tab. Formulas that refer to the table will be updated automatically when you change the table's name.

Do it!

C-5: Naming tables

Here's how	Here's why
1 In B4, type **=AVERAGE(**	Don't press Enter.
2 Select B7:B19	To select the Unit price column. The formula appears as shown in Exhibit 5-11.
Press (↵ ENTER)	To enter the formula. If you AutoFill the cell to the right, the next cell's formula will contain the adjacent table column's name.
3 AutoFill B4 one cell to the right	To copy the formula to C4.
From the AutoFill Options menu, choose **Fill Without Formatting**	To remove the currency formatting from C4.
Select C4 and observe the formula	*fx* =AVERAGE(Table1[Qty in stock])
	The formula uses Table1 as a reference. You'll now change the table name to see the effect this has on the formulas.
4 Select any cell in the table	
Click the **Design** tab	
5 In the Properties group, edit the Table Name box to read **InventoryTable**	Table Name: InventoryTable ·⬚· Resize Table
	Do not enter a space between words.
Select B4	*fx* =AVERAGE(InventoryTable[Unit price])
	The formula now refers to InventoryTable instead of Table1.
6 Update the workbook	

Functions tabulating row values

Explanation

Some Excel functions "expect" the arguments to be a range of cells. For example, the SUM function acts on a range of values, not just one. Therefore, an argument such as a table column name is valid for the SUM function; =SUM([January]) can be the equivalent of =SUM(C5:C14).

At times, however, you might want to use a table column name in a function, but reference only a single row. For example, if you want to sum the values across a table row, you don't want to sum all of the values for all of the rows. To address this issue, you can insert a special [@] argument in formulas.

Exhibit 5-12 shows this argument in a cell that sums the values in one row of the January-through-April columns of a table.

| f_x | =SUM(Table2[@[January]:[April]]) |

Exhibit 5-12: A function to sum a single row across table cells should include the [@] argument

Although you can type this argument, the easiest way to insert it is to use the AutoSum button to create the formula. Excel will then insert the argument automatically.

Do it!

C-6: Creating functions with the [@] argument

Here's how	Here's why
1 Click the **Sales** sheet	You'll convert this sheet's data to a table and then add a formula in a new column.
Select a cell in A4:F14 and define the range as a table	Click the Insert tab and click Table. Click OK to accept the defaults.
2 In G4, enter **Total**	Excel automatically adds this column to the table.
3 Click the **Home** tab	If necessary.
With G5 selected, click **AutoSum** in the Editing group	To add a formula that sums the values from the January-through-April columns.
Press (↵ ENTER)	To create the formula and automatically fill it to the remaining rows in the column.
	Next, you'll see the effect of removing the special [@] argument.
4 Edit the formula to read **=SUM(Table2[[January]:[April]])**	
	Delete the [@] argument from the formula.
Press (↵ ENTER)	When you press Enter, all cells in the column display the result $563,768, because all formulas are summing all of the values in the columns, not just the values to the cell's left.
On the Quick Access toolbar, click ↰	To return to the original formula in the filled cells.
Click ↰	To delete the remaining formula.
5 Update and close the workbook	

Unit summary: Tables

Topic A   In this topic, you identified records, fields, and field names as data components. You also **sorted** data based on the values in a column. You used the **AutoFilter** feature to show only those rows that meet certain criteria. Finally, you sorted and filtered data by using fill color and other cell attributes as the criteria.

Topic B   In this topic, you used the **Custom AutoFilter** dialog box to filter data based on multiple criteria. You used a criteria range and the **Advanced Filter** command to specify more complex criteria. You also copied filtered data to another location in the worksheet.

Topic C   In this topic, you created **tables** to simplify the tasks of formatting data, adding data, and creating formulas. You used **structured references** in formulas to include references to column names instead of A1-style ranges. You then renamed a table, and you used the **[@] argument** in a SUM function with column-name references to total only the cells in the same row.

Independent practice activity

In this activity, you'll sort and AutoFilter the values in a range of data. You'll also use a criteria range to filter the data, and copy the results to another place in the worksheet. Then, you'll define a range as a table, and use structured references to create formulas that refer to column names.

The files for this activity are in Student Data folder **Unit 5\Unit summary**.

1 Open Practice list and save it as **My practice list**.

2 Sort the data by Product code in ascending order. (*Hint:* Click the Data tab, select the first record in the Product Code field, and click Sort Smallest to Largest.)

3 Sort the data first by Re-order level (Kg) in descending order, and then by Product name in ascending order. (*Hint:* Click the Sort button to open the Sort dialog box.)

4 Use AutoFilter to display only those records for the supplier Cedric Stone. (There are only three.) Then display all records again.

5 Display only those records for the suppliers Cedric Stone or Bill Johnson. (There should be five records.) Then display all records again.

6 Filter the data to display only those records where the re-order level is greater than 2000 and less than 3500. (*Hint:* Click the AutoFilter button next to Re-order level (Kg) and choose **Number Filters**.)

7 Compare your results with Exhibit 5-13.

8 Turn off AutoFilter.

9 Use the criteria labels in F3:G3 to create a criteria range to display only those records where the re-order level for Cedric Stone is greater than 2000, or the re-order level for Bill Johnson is greater than 3000. (*Hint:* In F4, enter **Cedric Stone**; in G4, enter **>2000**; and so on. Select a cell in the original range and click Advanced in the Sort & Filter group. Select F3:G5 as the criteria range.)

10 Copy the filtered result to a range starting with I3 so that you can view the filtered and unfiltered data simultaneously. (*Hint:* Open the Advanced Filter dialog box and select "Copy to another location.")

11 Adjust column widths and row heights as necessary in the resulting range, and compare your results with Exhibit 5-14.

12 Click the Bonus sales sheet.

13 Define the data range as a table, and turn off the banded rows.

14 Add a Totals column starting in F4.

15 In the Totals column, create formulas to sum the four quarter values in each row. (*Hint:* Use the AutoSum button to insert the necessary arguments into the formula.)

16 Create a Total row, and select the SUM function from the list in cells B15:E15. (*Hint:* On the Design tab, check Total Row.) Compare your table to Exhibit 5-15.

17 Name the table **BonusSales**.

18 Update and close the workbook.

	Product name	Product code	Suppliers	Re-order level(K)
14	Basil leaf (ground)	20	Richie Hamond	3200
15	Caraway seed (ground)	14	Bill Johnson	3200
16	Cardamom seed (whole)	8	Anthony Felix	3000
17	Chives	31	Paul Michelin	3000
18	Cinnamon (ground) extra high oil (2x)	12	Anthony Felix	3000
19	Catnip leaf	26	Charles Nought	2900
20	Anise seeds	18	Bill Johnson	2800
21	Coarse kosher salt flakes	36	Henry Sanders	2800
22	Cassia	2	Garry Harper	2600
23	Anise	32	Cedric Stone	2500
24	Chinese star anise (whole)	27	Dennis Linekar	2500
25	Celery seed (ground)	12	Andy Howard	2300
26	Caraway seed (whole)	16	Michael Smith	2100
27	Cloves (whole)	35	Charly Bobbit	2100

Exhibit 5-13: The My practice list worksheet after Step 6

I Product name	J Product code	K Suppliers	L Re-order level(Kg)
Cardamom seed (ground)	5	Cedric Stone	4000
Caraway seed (ground)	14	Bill Johnson	3200
Anise	32	Cedric Stone	2500

Exhibit 5-14: The My practice list worksheet after Step 11

Product	Q	Q	Q	Q	Tot
Anise Seeds	$534	$423	$521	$625	$2,103
Asafoetida Powder	$654	$634	$326	$754	$2,368
Basil Leaf (Whole)	$6,778	$6,760	$4,568	$7,834	$25,940
Bay Leaf (Whole)	$233	$532	$525	$652	$1,942
Caraway Seed (Whole)	$354	$633	$422	$255	$1,664
Cardamom Seed (Whole)	$255	$525	$252	$624	$1,656
Cardamom Seed (Ground)	$422	$642	$642	$624	$2,330
Catnip Leaf	$854	$364	$474	$743	$2,435
Celery Seed (Whole)	$3,634	$6,344	$6,423	$2,546	$18,947
Chamomile Flowers	$356	$634	$632	$743	$2,365
Total	$14,074	$17,491	$14,785	$15,400	$61,750

Exhibit 5-15: The Bonus Sales worksheet after Step 16

Review questions

1 List the steps you would use to sort a range of data.

2 What command will display the AutoFilter arrows next to the column headings?

3 What is a criteria range?

4 List the steps you would use to keep an original range of data intact and place a copy of the filtered data somewhere else in the same worksheet.

5 How can formulas in a range that is defined as a table differ from those in a typical range?

6 Name two advantages of structured references.

Unit 6

Web and sharing features

Unit time: 30 minutes

Complete this unit, and you'll know how to:

A Save a workbook as a Web page, and use the AutoRepublish feature to keep the Web version of a workbook updated.

B Add and remove hyperlinks in a worksheet.

C Share workbooks via e-mail.

Topic A: Saving workbooks as Web pages

This topic covers the following Microsoft Office Specialist objectives for exam 77-882: Excel 2010.

#	Objective
1.3	**Personalize the environment by using Backstage**
	1.3.1 Manipulate the Quick Access Toolbar

Adding Web commands to the Quick Access toolbar

Explanation

By saving your workbooks, worksheets, and charts as Web pages, you can make them available to anyone who has a browser and access to the Internet or your corporate intranet. You can even provide some of Excel's functionality to people who don't have access to Excel, permitting these and other users to update and manipulate data through their browsers.

Web options are not displayed in the default Excel configuration, but you can add Web commands to the Quick Access toolbar. There are two ways to customize the Quick Access toolbar:

- Click the File tab and choose Options. Select Quick Access Toolbar. From the "Choose commands from" list, select the desired command, and click Add. The new command appears in the Customize Quick Access Toolbar list. Click OK.

- At the right end of the Quick Access toolbar, click the Customize arrow to display a list of commands, as shown in Exhibit 6-1. Select the desired command to add its button to the Quick Access toolbar.

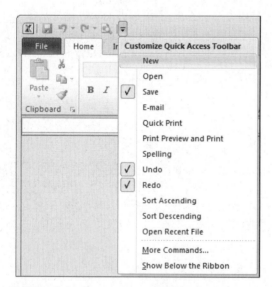

Exhibit 6-1: Customizing the Quick Access toolbar

Do it!   **A-1:   Making Web commands available**

Here's how	Here's why
1 On the right side of the Quick Access toolbar, click the arrow and choose **More Commands...**	To open the Excel Options dialog box with the Quick Access Toolbar settings displayed. You'll make a Web command available by adding it to the Quick Access toolbar.
2 Under Customize Quick Access Toolbar, verify that **For all documents (default)** is selected	You'll make these changes effective for all workbooks.
3 Under "Choose commands from," select **All Commands**	To display all available commands.
Select **Web Page Preview**	Near the bottom of the alphabetized list.
Click **Add**	To add a button for the Web Page Preview command to the Quick Access toolbar. You can change the order of the commands on the Quick Access toolbar by clicking the arrow buttons to the right of the command list.
4 Click **OK**	To save the changes and close the Excel Options dialog box.
5 Observe the Quick Access toolbar	The command button you added appears on the right side of the toolbar.

Saving workbooks

Explanation

You can save a selection, worksheet, or workbook as a Web page by using the Save As dialog box, shown in Exhibit 6-2. From the "Save as type" list, select Web Page, and then click OK. This saves the page with the file-name extension .htm. All of the graphics and images in the document are saved in an associated folder. You can also select Single File Web Page to save the page with the file-name extension .mht. This file type embeds the document's graphics and images directly in the Web page.

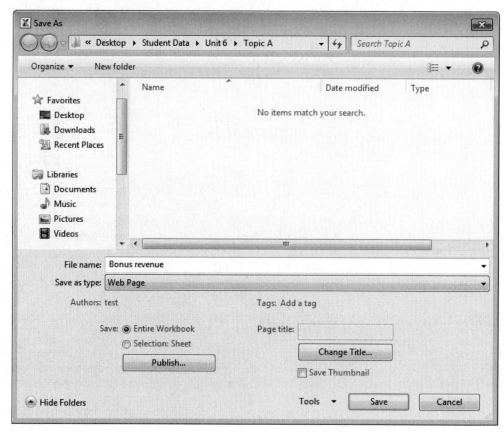

Exhibit 6-2: Using the Save As dialog box to save a workbook as a Web page

Previewing Web pages in a browser

You can preview Web pages in a Web browser before publishing them. When you open a Web page in a browser, that page is temporarily saved in the Windows directory. After you close the browser, the temporary files are deleted automatically.

To preview a Web page in a Web browser, click the Web Page Preview button that you added to the Quick Access toolbar. Your default Web browser will start automatically and display your Web page.

Do it!

A-2: Saving a workbook as a Web page

The files for this activity are in Student Data folder **Unit 6\Topic A**.

Here's how	Here's why
1 Open Bonus revenue	(From the current topic folder.) This workbook contains a sheet with four quarters of revenue figures for Outlander Spices. The sheet also contains an embedded chart.
2 Click [🔍]	(You added the Web Page Preview button to the Quick Access toolbar in the previous activity.) Internet Explorer opens, showing a preview of how the worksheet will look as a Web document. Though not all features of a published worksheet are available in the preview, it will give you an idea of how the worksheet will look when viewed in a browser.
Click [✕]	To close Internet Explorer.
3 Open the Save As dialog box	Click the File tab and choose Save As.
From the Save as type list, select **Web Page**	To save the file as a Web page. When you save a worksheet as a Web page, the Save As dialog box contains several unique options, as shown in Exhibit 6-2. You can choose to save the entire workbook or save only a selection, such as the current sheet or a selected range. You can also add a Web page title.
Save the file as **My bonus revenue**	To save the workbook as a Web page. A message box appears, stating that the Web page version of this file might contain features that are not compatible with the original.
Click **Yes**	To close the message box, if necessary.
4 Start Windows Explorer	Right-click Start and choose Open Windows Explorer. You can also click the Windows Explorer taskbar button.
Double-click **My bonus revenue**	(In the current topic folder.) To open it in Internet Explorer.
5 Click the information bar in the browser and choose **Allow Blocked Content...**	To remove security restrictions on this page. A Security Warning box prompts you to confirm that you'll let the page run active content.
Click **Yes**	To allow active content and close the Security Warning box.
6 Close Internet Explorer	

Publishing a Web page

Explanation

To control more aspects of how your worksheets or elements of them will behave on the Web, you can publish them. To publish a workbook or a part of it:

1 Open the Save As dialog box and select Web Page as the file type.

2 Click the Publish button to open the Publish as Web Page dialog box, shown in Exhibit 6-3.

3 From the Choose list, select the part you want to publish.

4 Click Publish to publish the worksheet and open the page in Internet Explorer, as shown in Exhibit 6-4.

The AutoRepublish feature

The AutoRepublish feature ensures that each time you save the data in a workbook that's published on the Web, the Web pages are also updated automatically. To use this feature, check the "AutoRepublish every time this workbook is saved" box in the Publish as Web Page dialog box. You can also disable AutoRepublish temporarily or permanently.

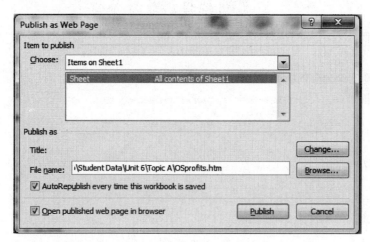

Exhibit 6-3: The Publish as Web Page dialog box

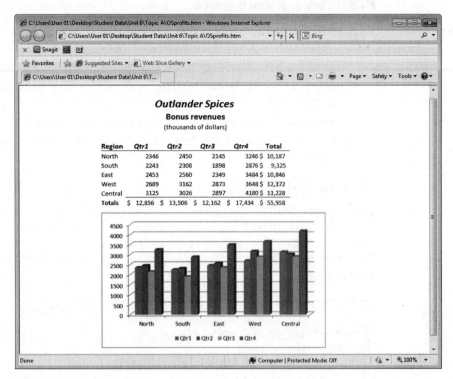

Exhibit 6-4: A published worksheet in Internet Explorer

A-3: Using the Publish as Web Page dialog box

Here's how	Here's why
1 Switch to My bonus revenue	Click the Excel taskbar button and choose My bonus revenue.
2 Open the Save As dialog box	
From the Save as type list, select **Web Page**	(If necessary.) To display the Web page options.
Click **Publish**	To open the Publish as Web Page dialog box.
3 Edit the File name box to read **OSprofits.htm**, as shown	File name: `\Student Data\Unit 6\Topic A\OSprofits.htm`
	For this class, you'll publish the Web page on your own hard drive. To make the file available to other users, you would need to publish it to a Web server or some other computer to which other users have access.
Check **AutoRepublish every time this workbook is saved**	To update the Web page with changes you make in your Excel file.
4 Check **Open published web page in browser**	(If necessary.) To get an immediate confirmation that the update works when you publish it.
5 Click **Publish**	To publish the worksheet on your own hard drive and open the page in Internet Explorer. Your screen should look similar to Exhibit 6-4.
6 Switch to the Excel window	
7 Change the value of E8 to **4000**	
8 Update the workbook	A message box appears.
Click **Yes**	To keep the workbook in this format. Another dialog box opens.
Select **Enable the AutoRepublish feature**	To make your worksheet changes appear on the Web page.
Click **OK**	To close the Microsoft Excel dialog box.

9 Switch to OSprofits.htm in
   Internet Explorer

   Click ⚡   To refresh the page and see that the change you
              made in Excel appears here as well.

   Close Internet Explorer

   Close the workbook

Topic B: Using hyperlinks

This topic covers the following Microsoft Office Specialist objectives for exam 77-882: Excel 2010.

#	Objective
2.3	**Apply and manipulate hyperlinks**
	2.3.1 Create a hyperlink in a cell
	2.3.2 Modify hyperlinks
	2.3.3 Modify hyperlinked cell attributes
	2.3.4 Remove a hyperlink

Inserting a hyperlink in a worksheet

Explanation

A *hyperlink* is any text or graphic that has been formatted to include a Uniform Resource Locator (URL). *URLs* are addresses of files on the Internet. When you click a hyperlink, your browser will load the file to which the URL points.

To insert a hyperlink in a worksheet:

1 Select the cell where you want the hyperlink to appear.
2 Click the Insert tab.
3 In the Links group, click Hyperlink to open the Insert Hyperlink dialog box.
4 Specify the text you want the link to display. This can be any text (but preferably something descriptive). It does not have to be the name of the file or its URL.
5 Specify the file or Web page to which you want the hyperlink to point. You can browse for a file or a Web page, or choose from recently used files, recently visited Web pages, or the current folder.
6 Click OK.

You can then click the hyperlink to load the specified file in your browser. If you save a worksheet as a Web page and that sheet contains a hyperlink, that link will work within the Web page as well.

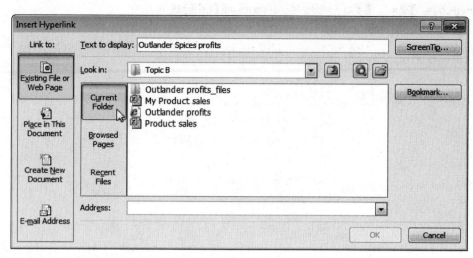

Exhibit 6-5: The Insert Hyperlink dialog box

Do it!

B-1: Inserting a hyperlink

The files for this activity are in Student Data folder **Unit 6\Topic B**.

Here's how	Here's why
1 Open Product sales	From the current topic folder
Save the workbook as **My Product sales**	You'll insert a hyperlink that points to the Web page.
2 Select A17	
3 Click the **Insert** tab	
4 In the Links group, click **Hyperlink**	To open the Insert Hyperlink dialog box.
5 In the Text to display box, enter **Outlander Spices profits**	The hyperlink will display this text.
Click **Current Folder**, as shown	To display the contents of the current folder.
6 Select **Outlander profits**	
Click **OK**	To insert the hyperlink in A17.
7 Point to the hyperlink	The shape of the pointer changes to a hand, and the ScreenTip displays the full path to the file.
Click the mouse button	The Outlander profits Web page opens in Internet Explorer. (A Security Notice might appear, reminding you that hyperlinks can be harmful to your computer and asking whether you want to continue.)
Close Internet Explorer	

8	Open the Save As dialog box	Click the File tab and choose Save As.
	From the Save as type list, select **Web Page**	
	Edit the File name box to read **my link**	File name: my link Save as type: Web Page
	Navigate to the current topic folder	If necessary.
9	Click **Save**	To save the file as a Web page. A message box may appear, stating that the file might contain features that are not compatible with Web pages.
	Click **Yes**	To save the file in this format while deleting any incompatible features, if necessary.

Modifying hyperlinks

Explanation

To edit a hyperlink:

1 Select the cell containing the hyperlink.
2 Right-click and choose Edit Hyperlink.
3 Modify the hyperlink as desired.
4 Click OK.

To select a cell containing a hyperlink without activating the link, use either of these techniques:

- Use the arrow keys to select the cell.
- Press and hold the mouse button until the mouse pointer changes from a pointing finger to a cross.

Removing a link versus deleting a link

You can right-click and choose Remove Hyperlink to clear a hyperlink; however, the text remains. This is useful when you have inserted a hyperlink using text in the worksheet. You can also remove a hyperlink by clicking the Remove Link button in the Edit Hyperlink dialog box.

When you press the Delete key, the cell contents are removed, including the hyperlink, the text, and any formatting that was applied to the cell.

Do it!

B-2: Modifying and deleting a hyperlink

The files for this activity are in Student Data folder **Unit 6\Topic B**.

Here's how	Here's why
1 Observe the title bar	The Web Page file "my link" is still open in Excel.
2 Right-click A17	The cell containing the hyperlink.
Choose **Edit Hyperlink...**	To open the Edit Hyperlink dialog box.
3 Edit the Text to display box to read **Outlander Spices Revenue**	Edit Hyperlink / Link to: / Text to display: Outlander Spices Revenue
In the Address box, verify that **Outlander profits.htm** is displayed	
Click **OK**	The hyperlink text has been changed.
4 Apply a border to A17	To apply an outline to the cell containing the hyperlink.
5 Update the Web page	Click the Save button.

6   Switch to Windows Explorer

    Open my link

Celery Seed (Whole)	$24,232	$28,437
Chamomile Flowers	$1,770	$2,591
Total	$72,899	$76,717

Outlander Spices Revenue

The hyperlink shown in Internet Explorer displays the edited text with a border.

    Click the hyperlink

To navigate to the Outlander profits Web page.

7   Switch to Excel

My link should still be open.

8   Right-click A17 and choose **Remove Hyperlink**

The link is removed, but the text and border remain.

9   Click ↺

To undo the last action.

    Press (DELETE)

To delete the hyperlink and the text. The border is still there.

    Update my link

Click Save.

10 Open my link in Internet Explorer

To verify that the hyperlink has been deleted.

11 Close Internet Explorer

Close all tabs, if prompted.

    Close my link

Topic C: Sharing workbooks

This topic covers the following Microsoft Office Specialist objectives for exam 77-882: Excel 2010.

#	Objective
7.1	**Share spreadsheets by using Backstage**
	7.1.1 Send a worksheet via E-mail or Skydrive

Using Save & Send

Explanation

Microsoft provides a variety of ways for you to share workbooks. You can e-mail a workbook as an attachment, save it to Windows Live on the Web, or save it to a SharePoint site.

To share a workbook file, click the File tab and then click Save & Send to display the sharing options, shown in Exhibit 6-6.

Option	Description
Send Using E-mail	Use e-mail to send the workbook as an attached file in Excel, PDF, or XPS format. You can also e-mail a link to the workbook or send the workbook as an Internet fax.
Save to Web	Save a copy of the workbook to the free online Windows Live storage site called SkyDrive. You can view and edit your Excel documents from any location by using a Web browser.
Save to SharePoint	Save a copy of the workbook to your organization's SharePoint site. Your system administrator configures a SharePoint site that provides a central location for people in the same company to view, copy, edit, and work together with files.

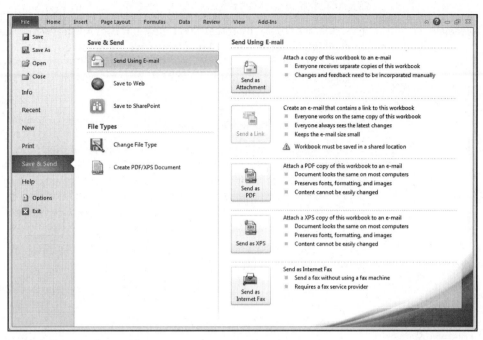

Exhibit 6-6: The Save & Send page

Do it!

C-1: Examining workbook sharing options

The files for this activity are in Student Data folder **Unit 6\Topic C**.

Here's how	Here's why
1 Open Outlander sales	
Save the workbook as **My outlander sales**	In the current topic folder.
2 Click the **File** tab and choose **Save & Send**	To display the Save & Send options, shown in Exhibit 6-6.
3 Observe the options for Send Using E-mail	You can send the workbook as an e-mail attachment in the original Excel file format, or send it as a different file type such as PDF or XPS.
4 Under Share, click **Save to Web**	You can use your Windows Live ID to access Windows Live SkyDrive, a free online storage site.
5 Examine the other sharing options	SharePoint enables you to publish Excel workbook files to a SharePoint site so that other people in your organization can use the files.
6 Close the workbook	

Sending workbooks via e-mail

Explanation

To send a workbook by e-mail, you must have a working e-mail account. It is not necessary that the sender and recipient have the same e-mail programs or the same version of Excel installed. In Excel 2010, you can save your workbook file in a backward-compatible format; however, some formatting might not be available in previous Excel formats.

Options for sharing workbooks through e-mail

You can share a workbook through e-mail either as an attachment or as a link. (To do the latter, you need Outlook 2000 or higher.) You must have a functioning e-mail account in order to e-mail workbooks as attachments or links. You do not have to use Microsoft Outlook as your e-mail application. To use another e-mail program, click Start and choose Default Programs. Click the link to "Set your default programs," and select the desired mail program as the default.

Using Outlook, here's how you send a workbook as an e-mail attachment:

1 Click the File tab and click Save & Send.

2 Click Send as Attachment. An e-mail message opens, with the current workbook inserted as an attachment.

3 Specify the address(es), and send the message.

Do it!

C-2: Using e-mail to send an attachment

Questions and answers
1 What options do you have for sending a workbook via e-mail?
2 What do you need to send a worksheet in the body of an e-mail message?
3 What are the steps for creating an e-mail message with the current workbook file inserted as an attachment?

Unit summary: Web and sharing features

Topic A   In this topic, you added the **Web Page Preview command** to the Quick Access toolbar and used this command to see the worksheet in a browser. You also saved a worksheet as a **Web page**. You then used the Publish as Web Page dialog box to save a worksheet with an embedded chart as a Web page. You also used the **AutoRepublish** feature.

Topic B   In this topic, you inserted and edited **hyperlinks** in a workbook. You learned that clicking a hyperlink opens a Web page in a browser.

Topic C   In this topic, you learned about different methods for **sharing** workbooks, and you learned how to send a workbook through e-mail.

Independent practice activity

In this activity, you'll publish workbooks as Web pages. You'll use AutoRepublish to update a published Web page when you change the source workbook. You'll add a hyperlink to a workbook, publish it as a Web page, and observe the link's action.

The files for this activity are in Student Data folder **Unit 6\Unit summary**.

1 Open Practice web 1 and save it as **My practice web 1**. This file contains bonus sales data for Outlander Spices' southern region.

2 Publish the workbook as a Web page. Name it **mysouthernregion.htm**, turn on the AutoRepublish feature, and save the file in the current Unit summary folder.

3 Open the Web page in your browser (if necessary).

4 Change the value in C6 to **7000** and update the workbook. To verify that the Web page was republished, switch to the browser and click Refresh. When finished, close the browser.

5 In Excel, open Practice web 2 and save it as **My practice web 2**. This file contains the northern region's sales data.

6 In A14, insert a hyperlink to the mysouthernregion.htm Web page. Make **Southern region** the text displayed for the hyperlink.

7 Publish My practice web 2 as a Web page. Name it **mynorthernregion.htm**, turn on AutoRepublish, and save the file in the current Unit summary folder.

8 Open mynorthernregion.htm in your browser (if necessary).

9 Use the hyperlink to open mysouthernregion.htm.

10 Update My practice web 2, enabling the AutoRepublish feature.

11 In A13 of the My practice web 1 workbook, insert a hyperlink to the mynorthernregion.htm Web page. Make **Northern region** the text displayed for the hyperlink.

12 Update the workbook.

13 Open mysouthernregion.htm in your browser, and compare it to Exhibit 6-7.

14 Use the hyperlink to load the mynorthernregion.htm Web page, and use the link in that page to reload mysouthernregion.htm.

15 Close the browser; then close all workbooks.

16 Update and close the workbooks.

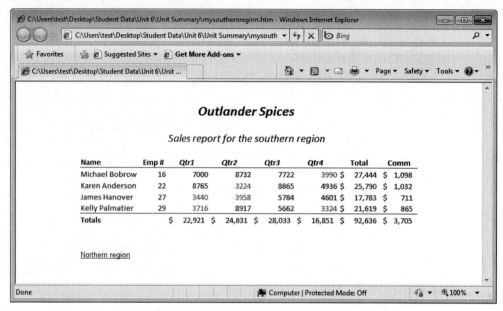

Exhibit 6-7: The contents of the mysouthernregion.htm Web page after Step 13

Review questions

1 When you save a worksheet as a Web page, you can save the file as a Single File Web Page with the extension .mht. When you use this option, how are the graphics and images stored?

2 When you save a worksheet as a Web page and save the file in HTML format, how are the graphics and images stored?

3 How can you preview a Web page in a Web browser?

4 List the steps you would use to publish a workbook.

5 What is a hyperlink?

Unit 7
Advanced charting

Unit time: 30 minutes

Complete this unit, and you'll know how to:

A Adjust the scale of a chart, and format data points.

B Create combination charts, trendlines, and sparklines to highlight different kinds of data.

C Add and modify drawing objects and shapes to highlight a specific portion of a chart, and add a picture to a worksheet.

Topic A: Chart formatting options

This topic covers the following Microsoft Office Specialist objective for exam 77-882: Excel 2010.

#	Objective
6.1	Create charts based on worksheet data

Changing a chart's scale

Explanation

Excel provides many formatting options for charts. You can use these options to represent or interpret complex data. For example, you can change the scale of a chart or format specific data points.

When you create or work with a chart, the Chart Tools appear. Design, Layout, and Format tabs are added to the Ribbon.

You can change the scale of a chart to:

- Adjust the range of values on each axis.
- Change the way the values appear on each axis.
- Specify the intervals at which the values appear.
- Set the point at which one axis crosses another.

To change the scale of a chart, select the value axis and click the Layout tab. In the Labels group, click Axes and choose Primary Vertical Axis, More Primary Vertical Axis Options to open the Format Axis dialog box. Click Axis Options to display the page shown in Exhibit 7-1. The following table describes some of the options on the Axis Options page:

Option	Specifies
Minimum	The lowest value on the value axis.
Maximum	The highest value on the value axis.
Major unit	The intervals for major tick marks and major gridlines on the value axis.
Minor unit	The intervals for minor tick marks and minor gridlines on the value axis.

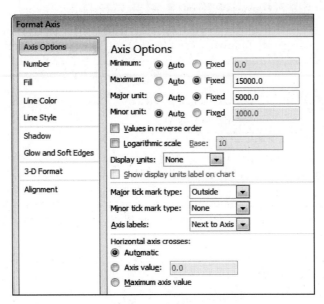

Exhibit 7-1: The Axis Options page in the Format Axis dialog box

Do it!

A-1: Adjusting the scale of a chart

The files for this activity are in Student Data folder **Unit 7\Topic A**.

Here's how	Here's why
1 Open Yearly bonus	
Save the workbook as **My yearly bonus**	In the current topic folder.
2 Verify that the Scale worksheet is active	It contains the quarterly bonus sales report for five Outlander Spices salespeople.

	On the chart, the value axis displays a maximum value of $15,000. The interval between the values is $5,000. This scale is not suitable because the value axis is too large, making the columns seem small and minimizing the difference between data points.
3 Select the chart	The Chart Tools appear on the Ribbon.
4 Click the **Layout** tab	On the Ribbon.
In the Axes group, click **Axes** and choose **Primary Vertical Axis, More Primary Vertical Axis Options...**	To open the Format Axis dialog box.
In the left-hand pane, select **Axis Options**	(If necessary.) You'll change the scale of the value axis.
5 Next to Maximum, select **Fixed**	(If necessary.) You'll override the current maximum value with your own fixed value.
Edit the Maximum box to read **10000**	Excel might reformat the values here with a single decimal place. The value you enter might appear as 10000.0.
Set the Major unit to **2000**	

Next to Major Unit, select Fixed, if necessary. Then edit the box to read 2000.

6 Click **Close**	To close the Format Axis dialog box and apply the new scale settings.

Deselect the chart

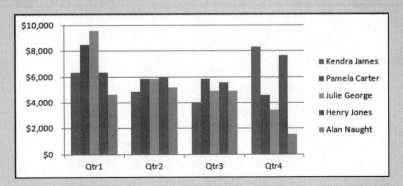

The value axis now displays a maximum value of $10,000. The major tick marks occur at intervals of $2,000. This scale is more appropriate for the data.

7 Update the workbook

Formatting data points

Explanation You can change the appearance of data points to make them stand out or make them easier to understand. You can add or remove labels, percentages, or leader lines. A *leader line* is a line from the data label to its associated data point. In a pie chart, you can change the orientation of the first slice or pull out a slice to make it stand out.

Labeling data points

To add a label to a data point:

1 Select the data point you want to label.

2 Click the Layout tab.

3 In the Labels group, click Data Labels and choose More Data Label Options to open the Format Data Label dialog box.

4 Click Label Options to display the corresponding page, as shown in Exhibit 7-2.

5 Select a label option and click Close.

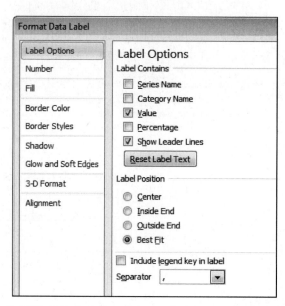

Exhibit 7-2: Label options in the Format Data Label dialog box

Formatting pie charts

You can format a pie chart to draw attention to specific data points. You can rotate the chart, and you can pull out a slice by dragging it away from the pie. The individual slice can be formatted to make it stand out from the rest of the chart.

Do it!   **A-2: Formatting a data point**

Here's how	Here's why
1 Click the **Datapoint** sheet	This worksheet contains the total yearly bonus sales report for several products. The pie chart represents a breakdown of sales by product.
2 Select the slice representing cinnamon sales	(Click the pie and then click the largest slice.) The Chart Tools tabs appear. You'll add a label to this data point.
3 Click the **Layout** tab	
In the Labels group, click **Data Labels** and choose **More Data Label Options...**	
	To open the Format Data Label dialog box. By default, Label Options is selected, as shown in Exhibit 7-2.
4 Under Label Contains, clear **Value**	You'll label the slice representing cinnamon sales as a percentage of the total.
Under Label Contains, check **Percentage**	
Under Label Position, select **Outside End**	To place the data label just outside the slice.
5 In the left pane, select **Number**	
From the Category list, select **Percentage**	To format the number as a percentage.
Edit the Decimal places box to read **0**	If necessary.
Click **Close**	To close the dialog box and add the label.
6 Observe the chart	
	The new data label, representing the total value of cinnamon sales, appears outside the pie slice.

7 Click anywhere in the chart	To deselect the slice and data label.
Point to the cinnamon slice	A ScreenTip appears, showing the total value of cinnamon sales and the percentage of total product sales it represents.
8 Select the slice representing cinnamon sales	You'll make other changes to the slice.
9 Click the **Format** tab	Under Chart Tools, on the Ribbon.
10 In the Current Selection group, click **Format Selection**	To open the Format Data Point dialog box. Series Options is selected by default.
11 Set the "Angle of first slice" value to **195**	

	(Drag the slider or type the value in the box.) To rotate the pie chart so that the cinnamon slice occupies a 9 o'clock position.
Set the Point Explosion value to approximately **20%**	To pull out the slice representing cinnamon sales so that it is separate from the rest of the pie chart and the data point stands out from the others.
12 In the left pane, select **3-D Format**	You'll give the slice some depth.
Under Bevel, click as shown	

You'll create a special effect for the slice.

Select the indicated bevel option

To create the effect of a raised circle.

13 Click **Close**   To close the dialog box.

Deselect the slice

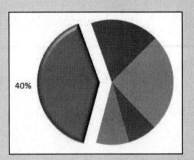

The slice now has a beveled edge to make it even more distinct from the other slices.

14 Update and close the workbook

Topic B: Combination charts

This topic covers the following Microsoft Office Specialist objectives for exam 77-882: Excel 2010.

#	Objective
6.4	**Apply Sparklines**
	6.4.1 Use Line chart types
	6.4.2 Use Column chart types
	6.4.3 Use Win/Loss chart types
	6.4.4 Create a Sparkline chart
	6.4.5 Customize a Sparkline
	6.4.6 Format a Sparkline
	6.4.7 Show or hide data markers

This topic covers the following Microsoft Office Specialist objectives for exam 77-888: Excel Expert 2010.

#	Objective
3.1	**Apply advanced chart features**
	3.1.1 Use Trend lines
	3.1.2 Use dual axes
	3.1.3 Use chart templates
	3.1.4 Use Sparklines

Changing chart types and adding axes

Explanation

You can combine two or more chart types in a single chart, called a *combination chart.* For example, you can combine a column chart with a line chart. Other chart combinations are also possible. You can use combination charts when you want to represent a wider range of information or when you want to highlight a series or the contrast between series. You can also graphically represent variations in data by using trendlines and sparklines.

At times, you might need to show two kinds of information on the same chart. For example, in Exhibit 7-3, the columns show expense and sales figures, measured in thousands of dollars, while the line shows profit figures, which are percentages. You can create combination charts by applying a secondary axis to one or more data series. You can also change the chart type for that data series to make it stand out from the rest of the chart. This is especially useful if the values for that data series are very different from the values for the other data series.

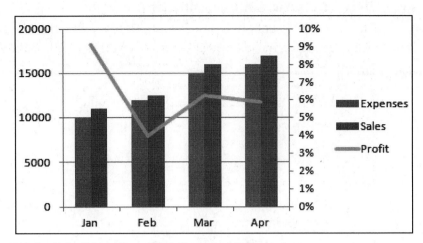

Exhibit 7-3: A sample column-line combination chart

To create a combination chart by changing the chart type of a data series:

1   Select the chart to display the Chart Tools tabs.

2   Click the Format tab.

3   In the Current Selection group, in the Chart Area list, select the data series for which you want to change the chart type.

4   Click the Design tab.

5   In the Type group, click Change Chart Type to open the Change Chart Type dialog box.

6   Select the chart type you want to apply to the selected data series.

7   Click OK.

To create a combination chart that uses a secondary value axis:

1   Select the chart and click the Format tab.

2   In the Current Selection group, in the Chart Area list, select the data series that will use the secondary value axis.

3   In the Current Selection group, click Format Selection to open the Format Data Series dialog box.

4   Under Plot Series On, select Secondary Axis.

5   Click Close.

Do it!

B-1:   Creating a combination chart

The files for this activity are in Student Data folder **Unit 7\Topic B**.

Here's how	Here's why
1 Open Profit trends	
Save the workbook as **My profit trends**	In the current topic folder.
Click the **Combination** sheet	This sheet displays profit trends for four months.

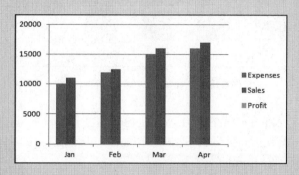

	The category axis represents the months, and the value axis represents the sales. Profit columns are not visible because the Profit values are too small relative to the Expenses and Sales values.
2 Select the chart	
3 Click the **Format** tab	
In the Current Selection group, from the Chart Area list, select **Series "Profit"**	

Chart Area
- Chart Area
- Horizontal (Category) Axis
- Legend
- Plot Area
- Vertical (Value) Axis
- Vertical (Value) Axis Major Gridlines
- Series "Expenses"
- Series "Sales"
- Series "Profit"

	You'll create a secondary value axis to represent the Profit data series.
4 Click **Format Selection**	To open the Format Data Series dialog box. Series Options is selected by default.
5 Under Plot Series On, select **Secondary Axis**	To insert a secondary axis on the right side of the chart.
Click **Close**	To close the dialog box. The secondary axis appears on the right side of the chart. The chart columns for the Profit data series overlap the other columns.
6 Click the **Design** tab	

7 In the Type group, click **Change Chart Type**	To display the Change Chart Type gallery. You'll assign a separate chart type to the Profit data series so that it will be represented as a line.
In the Chart Type list, select **Line**	
8 In the Line gallery, click as shown	
	To select the first chart type under Line.
Click **OK**	To close the gallery and change the chart type for the Profit data series from column to line, as shown in Exhibit 7-3. Now it's easier to understand how profit percentages fluctuate with respect to expenses and sales.
9 Update the workbook	

Adding trendlines

Explanation

You can create a trendline in a chart to emphasize the pattern of change in your data. *Trendlines* are graphical representations of drifts or variations in a data series. Trendlines can highlight important variations and make your charts easier to understand, and they can facilitate forecasting and decision making.

To add a trendline to a chart:

1 Select the chart or data series to which you want to add a trendline.
2 Click the Layout tab.
3 In the Analysis group, click Trendline.
4 From the menu, choose the type of trendline you want to apply.

Do it!   **B-2:   Creating a trendline**

Here's how	Here's why
1 Click the **Trendline** sheet	

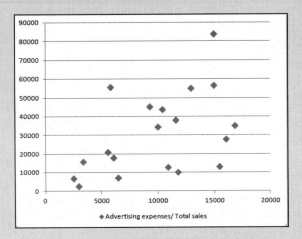

	It shows the advertising expenses and total sales for several years. In the chart, it's difficult to determine whether sales increased or decreased relative to changes in advertising expenses.
2 Select the chart	You'll create a trendline for the Advertising Expenses/Total Sales data series.
3 Click the **Layout** tab	
4 In the Analysis group, click **Trendline** and choose **Linear Trendline**	To display the trendline on the chart. The trendline indicates that total sales increased as advertising expenses did.

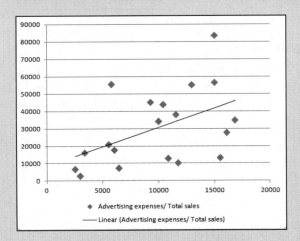

5 Update the workbook

Sparklines

Explanation

A new feature in Excel 2010 is the ability to add sparklines to worksheets. A *sparkline* is a small chart that is inserted into a single cell to illustrate a pattern or trend in data. There are three types of sparklines: line, column, and win/loss. A sparkline chart resides in the background of a cell, so you can enter text on top of it.

Inserting sparkline

Sparklines can be inserted anywhere in a worksheet. However, it's recommended that they be adjacent to the data they are representing.

To insert a sparkline:

1   Select the cell(s) where you want to insert the sparkline.
2   Click the Insert tab.
3   In the Sparklines group, click the desired Sparkline button (Line, Column, or Win/Loss) to open the Create Sparklines dialog box, shown in Exhibit 7-4.
4   In the Data Range box, enter the range to be charted. Use the Collapse dialog box button, if necessary. **Note:** You can select multiple rows of data to create multiple sparklines at once.
5   In the Location Range box, verify that the destination is correct.
6   Click OK.

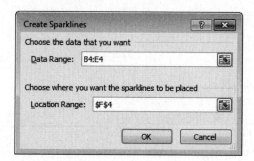

Exhibit 7-4: The Create Sparklines dialog box

Modifying sparklines

To modify a sparkline chart, use the buttons on the Sparkline Tools | Design tab. As with any other Excel charts, you can modify a sparkline by changing its type, applying a different style, changing the color or line weight, or showing data points and markers.

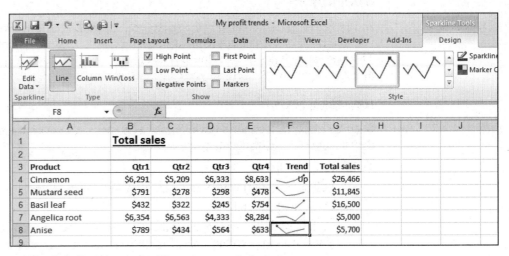

Exhibit 7-5: Inserting sparklines in a worksheet

Do it!

B-3:   Inserting sparklines

Here's how	Here's why
1 Click the **Sales** sheet	You'll create sparklines that provide a visual representation of the sales figures.
2 Insert a column between columns E and F	
3 In F3, enter **Trend**	To give the new column a heading.
4 Select F4	You can insert sparklines anywhere in the worksheet; however, it's recommended that you keep them adjacent to the data they depict.
Click the **Insert** tab	The Sparklines group provides three types of sparklines: Line, Column, and Win/Loss. The type you use depends on what you are trying to illustrate.
In the Sparklines group, click **Line**	The Create Sparklines dialog box opens.

5 In the Data Range box, enter **B4:E4**

Create Sparklines
B4:E4

If necessary, collapse the dialog box to select the range in the worksheet. You can also type directly in the Data Range box.

6 In the Location Range box, verify that F4 is specified

Choose where you want the sparklines to be placed
Location Range: $F$4

By default, the location is entered as an absolute reference.

   Click **OK**

To create a sparkline in cell F4. The sparkline chart illustrates the upward trend of cinnamon sales from the first to the last quarter.

7 Select F4

If necessary.

Drag to fill the sparkline down to F8

Qtr4	Trend	T
,633		
$478		
$754		
,284		
$633		

Sparklines appear in the range. The AutoFill options handle appears, as shown.

8 Select F4

f_x	

To see the empty formula bar. Because sparklines reside in the background of the cell, the formula bar remains empty.

In cell F4, enter **Up**

Trend	Total sales
Up	$26,466
	$11,845
	$16,500
	$5,000
	$5,700

To enter text in the cell and see that it appears on top of the sparkline.

9	Select F4:F8	As shown in Exhibit 7-5, the Sparkline Tools | Design tab is activated. As with other Excel charts, you can change the style and appearance of sparklines.
	In the Style gallery, explore the various styles	You can change the style of the sparkline, if you wish.
10	In the Type group, click **Column**	To change the sparkline chart type to Column.
	Click **Win/Loss**	To change the type to Win/Loss.
	Change the sparkline chart type back to **Line**	In the Type group, click Line.
11	In the Show group, check **High Point**	A marker is added to the highest point in each sparkline. You can add markers for the highest, lowest, first, last, or negative point or for all individual points. Use the Marker Color menu to change the marker colors.
12	Deselect the sparklines	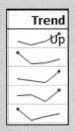 You can clearly see the new sparklines with the highest-point markers, as shown in Exhibit 7-5.
13	Update and close the workbook	

Chart templates

Explanation

Microsoft provides chart templates that you can use to create charts. You can save time by using chart templates because the formatting has already been done for you.

To download a chart template:

1 Click the File tab and choose New.
2 Under Office.com Templates, open the More templates folder.
3 Click the Charts folder. A listing of the available chart templates is displayed.
4 Select the desired chart template and click Download.
5 The downloaded chart appears on the worksheet with sample data.
6 Modify the data as desired. The chart automatically updates.

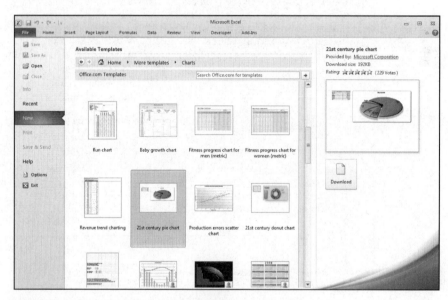

Exhibit 7-6: Downloading a chart template

Saving a chart as a template

You can also save a formatted chart as a template. To do so, select the chart and click Save as Template on the Chart Tools | Design tab. Enter a file name and click Save. By default, the new template will be saved in the Templates/Chart folder and will be available like other Excel charts.

Do it!

B-4:   Using a chart template

The files for this activity are in Student Data folder **Unit 7\Topic B**.

Here's how	Here's why
1 On the File tab, choose **New**	
2 Under Office.com Templates, click the **More Templates** folder	You'll download a chart template from Office.com.
Click **Back**	(If necessary.) To reload the templates lists.
Click **Charts and diagrams**	A list containing thumbnails of the available chart templates appears.
Click **Business charts**	
Scroll down and select **21st century pie chart**	As shown in Exhibit 7-6.
3 Click **Download**	The pie chart is downloaded and displayed on the worksheet named Assets. The default workbook name is PieChart1, and sample data appears to the left of the chart.
4 In the sample data table, edit any asset name or amount	To see your changes reflected in the chart.
5 Save the workbook as **My PieChart1**	
Close the workbook	

Topic C: Graphical elements

This topic covers the following Microsoft Office Specialist objectives for exam 77-882: Excel 2010.

#	Objective
6.2	**Apply and manipulate illustrations**
	6.2.6 Modify Shape
6.3	**Create and modify images by using the Image Editor**
	6.3.1 Make corrections to an image
	6.3.1.1 Sharpen or soften an image
	6.3.1.2 Change brightness
	6.3.1.3 Change contrast

Drawing objects

Explanation

You can highlight a specific portion of a chart by adding graphical elements, such as text boxes, lines, and arrows. You can also format these elements to make them stand out or fit in better.

When you create or work with a shape, the Drawing Tools appear, adding a Format tab to the Ribbon.

You can use the Shapes gallery to insert lines, arrows, shapes, and 3-D objects in the chart area. To add a shape to a chart:

1   Select the chart and click the Layout tab.

2   In the Insert group, click Shapes to display the Shapes gallery.

3   Select the desired shape and drag within the chart to create that shape.

You can also use the Insert group to create drawing objects such as text boxes. To create a text box:

1   Click the Layout tab.

2   In the Insert group, click Text Box. The pointer changes to a thin arrow pointing downward.

3   Point to where you want to place the text box, and drag to create the box.

Do it!

C-1:   Adding graphical elements

The files for this activity are in Student Data folder **Unit 7\Topic C**.

Here's how	Here's why
1 Open Revenue comparison	
Save the workbook as **My revenue comparison**	
2 Select the chart	
Click the **Layout** tab	
3 In the Insert group, click **Text Box**	
Drag to create a text box outside the chart	The Drawing Tools | Format tab appears on the Ribbon. You'll move and resize the box.
4 Move the text box as shown	Drag it onto the chart.
5 Click in the text box and type **Sales hike**	You'll emphasize the steep rise in sales in the third quarter.
6 Resize the box to better fit the text	

7 Select the text

Right-click the selected text

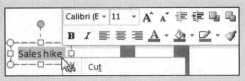

The Mini toolbar appears above the shortcut menu. You can change the font, font size, typestyle, and colors here.

On the Mini toolbar, click

To apply the italic style to the selected text.

8 Click the **Format** tab

Under Drawing Tools, on the Ribbon.

9 In the Insert Shapes group, click as shown

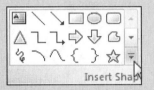

(The More button.) To display the Shapes gallery.

In the Shapes gallery, click as shown

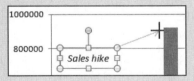

To select the Arrow line. The pointer takes the shape of a crosshair that you can use to draw an arrow.

10 Point to the upper-right corner of the text in the text box

The foot of the arrow will be here.

Drag as shown

To create an arrow pointing from the text box to the tallest column of the chart. The text and the arrow emphasize the steep rise in sales.

Click outside the chart area

To observe the text box and arrow. You'll format the line in the next activity.

11 Update the workbook

Formatting graphical elements

Explanation

You can change the shape, size, or color of graphical elements. Here's how:

1   Double-click the graphical element you want to format.
2   On the Format tab, in the Shape Styles group, click either the Shape Fill, Shape Outline, or Shape Effects button to display a corresponding menu.
3   Choose an option from the menu. Some menu options display galleries, as shown in Exhibit 7-7.

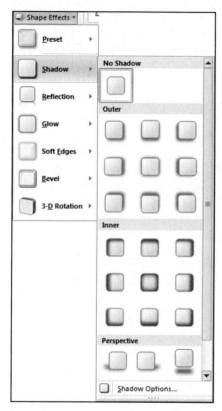

Exhibit 7-7: The Shadow gallery accessed from the Shape Effects menu

Do it!

C-2: Formatting a graphical element

Here's how	Here's why
1 Double-click the Sales hike arrow	To activate the Drawing Tools | Format tab.
2 In the Shape Styles group, click **Shape Effects**	To display a menu.
Choose **Shadow**	To display a gallery of shadow effects, as shown in Exhibit 7-7.
Point to the various effect options	To see a Live Preview of how the effects will look.
Click anywhere outside the Shadow gallery	To close it.
3 In the Shape Styles group, click **Shape Outline**	To display shape options.
Point to **Arrows**	To display the Arrows gallery. The current arrowhead style is highlighted.
Click as shown	 To apply Arrow Style 5 to the arrow in the chart.
4 Display the shape options again	Click Shape Outline.
Above Theme Colors, choose **Automatic**	To change the color of the arrow to black.
5 Update the workbook	

Adding pictures

Explanation

You can add a picture to a worksheet to emphasize a specific point or add new information, as shown in Exhibit 7-8. You can insert pictures from the Clip Organizer or from files, or you can import pictures directly from a digital camera or scanner. After you have inserted a picture, you can move, resize, and delete it just as you would any other object.

To insert a picture from a file:

1 Select a cell in the worksheet.
2 Click the Insert tab.
3 In the Illustrations group, click Picture to open the Insert Picture dialog box.
4 Open the folder that contains the picture.
5 Select the picture and click Insert.

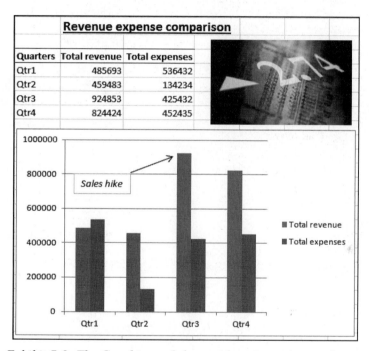

Exhibit 7-8: The Graphic worksheet with a picture inserted

Do it!

C-3:   Adding a picture to a worksheet

The files for this activity are in Student Data folder **Unit 7\Topic C**.

Here's how	Here's why
1 Select E7	You'll insert a picture.
2 Click the **Insert** tab	
3 In the Illustrations group, click **Picture**	To open the Insert Picture dialog box.
4 Navigate to the current topic folder	Student Data folder Unit 7\Topic C.
Select **Profits**	
Click **Insert**	(You might need to scroll to view the picture.) To insert the picture. The Picture Tools	Format tab is active. The picture is large, so you'll crop and resize it.
5 Update the workbook	

Modifying pictures

Explanation

When you insert or work with a picture, the Picture Tools appear, adding a Format tab to the Ribbon.

Resizing a picture

To resize a picture, you must first select it by clicking it. Then point to one of the sizing handles at the corners of the picture frame. The mouse pointer changes to a double-sided arrow. Drag the sizing handle to resize the picture.

To resize a picture proportionally, press and hold Shift before dragging the sizing handle. This forces the picture's height and width to resize at the same rate.

Modifying a picture

To move a picture, select it and drag it to a new location on the worksheet. If you want to move the picture to another worksheet or workbook, click the Home tab. In the Clipboard group, click Cut. Then navigate to the destination worksheet or workbook and paste the picture.

You can use the buttons on the Picture Tools | Format tab to rotate or crop a picture. Any picture in Excel can be cropped, except for animated GIFs.

You can adjust a picture's brightness and contrast by using the Corrections button in the Adjust group on the Picture Tools | Format tab.

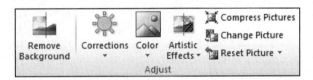

Exhibit 7-9: The Adjust group

Do it!

C-4:   Modifying a picture

The files for this activity are in Student Data folder **Unit 7\Topic C**.

Here's how	Here's why
1 In the Size group, click **Crop**	The pointer changes to an arrow with a cropping symbol.
2 Point to the upper-middle edge of the picture, and drag down as shown	To crop the top portion of the picture. While the pointer is in Crop mode, dragging the corners or the middle edges crops the picture.

3 Click **Crop**	To exit Crop mode. The pointer changes.
4 Observe the Size group	The Height and Width boxes display the dimensions of the picture.
5 Press and hold (SHIFT)	
While holding (SHIFT), drag the lower-right handle up and to the left	To proportionally resize the picture.
Release (SHIFT)	
6 Observe the Height and Width boxes	In the Size group. The boxes display the new dimensions of the picture.
Resize the picture proportionally to approximately 1.25" in height and 2.25" in width	Press and hold Shift, and drag a handle. Release Shift, and observe the dimensions in the Size group. Repeat as necessary.
7 Drag the picture to the right of the data	As shown in Exhibit 7-8.
8 In the Adjust group, click **Corrections**	To display the Sharpen & Soften and Brightness and Contrast galleries.
Point to each value in the menu, while observing the picture	The Live Preview function displays the effect of changing the picture's brightness and contrast.

Press (ESC)	To close the menu.
Deselect the picture	(Click any blank cell.) To close the Picture Tools | Format tab.
9 Update and close the workbook	

Unit summary: Advanced charting

Topic A   In this topic, you adjusted the **scale** of a chart and formatted data points. You added **data labels**, such as the percentage value of a data point, to a chart. You also exploded a slice in a pie chart.

Topic B   In this topic, you created a **combination chart** by using two value axes. You also added **trendlines**, which can be used to highlight the variations of data in a data series. Finally, you created **sparklines** to illustrate trends or patterns.

Topic C   In this topic, you added and formatted **drawing objects** and shapes, which can be used to emphasize a specific point in a chart. You also added **pictures** to a worksheet and learned how to modify images by sharpening them and changing the brightness or contrast.

Independent practice activity

In this activity, you'll change the values on the horizontal axis, change the maximum scale of the value axis, add a text box and arrow, and add a linear trendline.

The files for this activity are in Student Data folder **Unit 7\Unit summary**.

1 Open Practice charts and save it as **My practice charts**.

2 Click the Bonus sales worksheet, if necessary.

3 Change the category (horizontal) axis values to read **Q1**, **Q2**, **Q3**, **Q4**. (*Hint:* The values are in column A of the data.)

4 Change the maximum scale value of the value axis to **250**.

5 Add a text box to the worksheet, and enter **Lowest sales** in the box. Resize the box and the text to fit, apply the bold style, and then drag the text box onto the chart, as shown in Exhibit 7-10.

6 Add an arrow leading from the text box to the column showing the lowest sales. Apply Arrow Style 9 and the color black to the arrow.

7 Compare your chart with Exhibit 7-10.

8 Create a linear trendline for the data in the Trends worksheet.

9 Update and close the workbook.

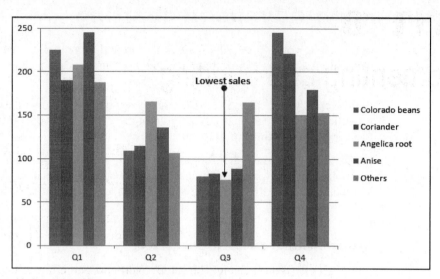

Exhibit 7-10: The chart after Step 6

Review questions

1 How can you change the scale of a chart?

2 What is a leader line?

3 What is a combination chart?

4 What is a trendline?

5 List the steps you would use to insert a picture from a file.

6 Which of the following best describes a sparkline?

    A A graphical representation of trends in data

    B A small chart in a single cell that shows patterns in data

    C An animated SmartArt graphic

    D A line connecting data labels to their respective data points

Unit 8

Documenting and auditing

Unit time: 60 minutes

Complete this unit, and you'll know how to:

A Use auditing features to trace precedent and dependent cells, and trace errors.

B Add and edit comments for a cell and a worksheet.

C Protect a workbook or part of a worksheet from unauthorized access or unintentional changes.

D Share workbooks, merge versions of a workbook, track changes made by various users, remove personal data from a workbook, and mark a workbook as final.

Topic A: Auditing features

This topic covers the following Microsoft Office Specialist objectives for exam 77-888: Excel Expert 2010.

#	Objective
2.1	**Audit formulas**
	2.1.1 Trace formula problems
	2.1.2 Trace dependents
	2.1.3 Trace errors
	2.1.5 Locate invalid formulas
	2.1.6 Correct errors in formulas

Tracing cell values

Explanation

You might want to identify the cells on which the value of a formula is based. Excel provides formula auditing commands, such as Trace Precedents and Trace Dependents, to point out such cells.

A *precedent cell* provides data to a specific cell. A *dependent cell* relies on the value of another cell. When you click the Trace Precedents and Trace Dependents buttons in the Formula Auditing group on the Formulas tab, Excel draws arrows showing precedent and dependent cells.

Do it!

A-1: Tracing precedent and dependent cells

The files for this activity are in Student Data folder **Unit 8\Topic A**.

Here's how	Here's why
1 Open Inventory	
Save the workbook as **My inventory**	In the current topic folder. The Monthly QOH worksheet contains a single month's quantity-on-hand totals for seven products.
2 Observe that the worksheet displays error values in some cells	These error values are indicated by the green triangles that appear in the upper-left corner of the cells.
3 Select C10	This cell contains the formula =D10/B10.
4 Click the **Formulas** tab	

In the Formula Auditing group, click **Trace Precedents**

Price/Unit	Total	Total
2.50	1513	3782.50
1.75	4873	8527.50
2.00	7507	15014.00
1.50	3694	5541.00
1.25	5265	6581.25

To trace the precedent cells of the selected cell. You can see two tracer arrows meeting at C10. These indicate that B10 and D10 provide values for the formula in C10 and are the precedent cells of C10.

5 In the Formula Auditing group, click **Remove Arrows** — To hide all tracer arrows.

6 Click **Trace Dependents**

Total	Total	Opening	Closing
1513	3782.50	3484	1971
4873	8527.50	6000	1127
7507	15014.00	8000	493
3694	5541.00	4143	449
5265	6581.25	7343	2078
#DIV/0!	6042.40	6782	#DIV/0!
1118	2012.40	3676	2558
			#DIV/0!

To trace the dependent cells of C10. Tracer arrows point from C10 to F10 and F14. The calculated values of F10 and F14 get their data from C10 and are the dependent cells of C10.

7 Hide the tracer arrows — Click Remove Arrows.

8 Update the workbook

Tracing errors in a worksheet

Explanation

When Excel detects an error, it displays an error value (in the cell) and an Error Checking button. You can click this button to display a menu of commands that can help you trace and correct the error. The Formula Auditing group on the Formulas tab also provides tools for this.

To trace an error, select the cell that contains the error; then, in the Formula Auditing group, click the arrow on the Error Checking button and choose Trace Error. You'll see tracer arrows pointing from the cell containing the error to other cells that provide values for the formula. An error in a cell might be caused by a reference to another cell that also contains an error. If so, a red arrow points to that cell. Blue arrows point from the cell where the error originates to the sources of that cell's formula.

Do it!   **A-2:   Tracing errors**

Here's how	Here's why
1 Select F14	
2 In the Formula Auditing group, click the Error Checking arrow and choose **Trace Error**	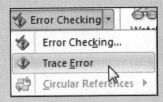

To display tracer arrows that show the source of the error produced by the formula in F14.

3 Observe the worksheet

Price/Unit	Total	Total	Opening	Closing
2.50	1513	3782.50	3484	1971
1.75	4873	8527.50	6000	1127
2.00	7507	15014.00	8000	493
1.50	3694	5541.00	4143	449
1.25	5265	6581.25	7343	2078
	#DIV/0!	6042.40	6782	#DIV/0!
1.80	1118	2012.40	3676	2558
				#DIV/0!

A red arrow points from C12 to F14. This arrow indicates that the cause of the error is the invalid value in C12. C12 gets its value from B12 and D12, as indicated by the blue arrows. B12 is empty, which causes the invalid value in C12.

4 In B12, enter **2**

Price/Unit	Total	Total	Opening	Closing
2.50	1513	3782.50	3484	1971
1.75	4873	8527.50	6000	1127
2.00	7507	15014.00	8000	493
1.50	3694	5541.00	4143	449
1.25	5265	6581.25	7343	2078
2.00	3021.2	6042.40	6782	3760.8
1.80	1118	2012.40	3676	2558
				2436.9429

To correct the error values. The red arrow disappears, and valid numeric values replace the error values. The blue arrows indicate non-error conditions.

5 Hide the tracer arrows

6 Update and close the workbook

Topic B: Comments in cells and workbooks

This topic covers the following Microsoft Office Specialist objectives for exam 77-882: Excel 2010.

#	Objective
1.3	**Personalize the environment by using Backstage**
	1.3.3 Manipulate Excel default settings (Excel Options)
	1.3.4 Manipulate workbook properties (Document Panel)
2.1	**Construct cell data**
	2.1.1 Use Paste Special
	2.1.1.8 Comments
7.2	**Manage comments**
	7.2.1 Insert
	7.2.2 View
	7.2.3 Edit
	7.2.4 Delete comments

Viewing comments

Explanation

A *comment* is a note or annotation that you can add to cells or workbooks to provide additional information. Adding comments to data makes your worksheet easier for other users to interpret. These comments do not alter the data in the cell.

Comments in cells are denoted by small, red triangles, called *comment indicators*, in the upper-right corner of the cells. To view a comment, point to the cell containing the comment indicator. To show all comments simultaneously, click the Review tab; then, in the Comments group, click Show All Comments. Click the button again to hide all comments.

Do it!

B-1: Viewing comments in a worksheet

The files for this activity are in Student Data folder **Unit 8\Topic B**.

Here's how	Here's why
1 Open Quantity	
Save the workbook as **My quantity**	In the current topic folder.
2 Observe C9	7507
	There is a red comment indicator in the upper-right corner of the cell.
3 Point to C9	4873 User01: 7507 Highest units sold across 3694 months
	To display the associated comment. By default, cells always display comment indicators but do not display comments until you point to the cells.
Point to another cell	The comment disappears.
4 Click the **Review** tab	
5 In the Comments group, click **Show All Comments**	To display all comments.

Price/Unit	Total	Total	Opening	Closing
2.50	User01:	1:	484	1971
1.75	Price reduced by	t units sold across	000	1127
2.00	10%		000	493
1.50	3694	5541.00	4143	449
1.25	5265	6581.25	7343	2078
2.00	3021.2	6042.40	User01:	
1.80	1118	2012.40	Sales have suffered because of competition with another brand	

6 Click **Show All Comments**	To hide all the comments.

Adding and managing cell comments

Explanation

Comments can be added to cells and edited as needed.

To add a comment, select a cell and click the Review tab. In the Comments group, click New Comment; then enter your text in the comment box that appears.

To edit a comment, select the cell containing the comment you want to edit. Click Edit Comment in the Comments group, or right-click the cell and choose Edit Comment. When you're finished making changes, click outside the comment box.

To delete a comment, either select the cell and click Delete in the Comments group, or right-click the cell and choose Delete Comment from the shortcut menu.

To paste only comments, right-click the cell containing the comment you want to copy and choose Copy. Then right-click the destination cell and choose Paste Special. In the Paste Special dialog box, select Comments and click OK.

Comment display options

By using the Excel Options dialog box, you can customize the way comments and comment indicators appear. You can display only indicators, both comments and indicators, or nothing at all. The default setting displays only the comment indicators, and displays a comment when you point to a cell. When you change the comment indicator settings, the new settings will be applied to all new workbooks.

Do it!   **B-2:   Adding a comment to a cell**

Here's how	Here's why
1 Select E9	
2 In the Comments group, click **New Comment**	
	Your user name appears in the comment box. The red comment indicator appears in the upper-right corner of the cell.
Type **The decision to begin with a high opening stock worked.**	To add this information as a comment.
Click outside the comment box	The comment box disappears, but the cell displays the red comment indicator.
3 Point to E9	
	To view the comment you just added.
4 Click the **File** tab and choose **Options**	To open the Excel Options dialog box. You'll view the display options for cell comments.
In the category list, select **Advanced**	
Under Display, observe the "For cells with comments, show" options	These settings determine whether and how comments and their indicators are displayed. Changes made here affect this workbook and all new workbooks.
Click **Cancel**	To close the dialog box.
5 Select E9	You'll edit the comment you just added.
In the Comments group, click **Edit Comment**	To open the comment in Edit mode.
Change **The** to **Our**	

6	Click another cell	To close the comment and apply the edit. The comment reflects the change.
7	Right-click E9	You'll copy this comment to the adjacent cell D9.
	Choose **Copy**	
8	Right-click D9 and choose **Paste Special...**	To open the Paste Special dialog box.
	Under Paste, select **Comments**	

Paste
- ○ All
- ○ Formulas
- ○ Values
- ○ Formats
- ◉ Comments
- ○ Validation

	Click **OK**	The comment has been pasted in D9 while the value remains the same.
9	Right-click E9	To display a shortcut menu.
	Choose **Delete Comment**	To delete the comment.
10	Update the workbook	

Adding workbook comments

Explanation

You can add a comment to a workbook by using the Document Panel, shown in Exhibit 8-1. This panel can also be used to enter workbook data, such as a descriptive title, a subject, an author name, a company name, and keywords.

To add comments and other information to an open workbook:

1   Click the File tab and choose Info.
2   Click Properties and choose Show Document Panel. The Document Properties Panel is displayed at the top of the workbook window.
3   Enter descriptive information in the appropriate boxes.
4   Close the Document Panel.

You can point to a workbook file in Windows Explorer to display a ScreenTip that contains some of the workbook properties. This ScreenTip also appears when you point to a workbook file in Excel's Open and Save dialog boxes.

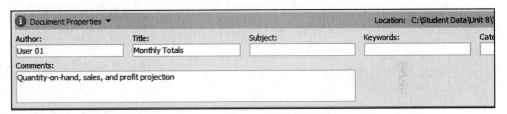

Exhibit 8-1: The Document Panel appears below the Ribbon

Do it!

B-3: Adding comments to a workbook

The files for this activity are in Student Data folder **Unit 8\Topic B**.

Here's how	Here's why
1 Click the **File** tab and choose **Info**	The right side of the Info page displays a thumbnail of the active file and some of its properties. You'll add a comment to this workbook file.
Click **Properties** and choose **Show Document Panel**	To open the Document Panel, below the Ribbon.
2 In the Author box, enter your name	By default, the Author box is populated with the user name that first created the file. Change it to your own name.
In the Title box, enter **Monthly Totals**	
3 In the Comments box, enter **Quantity-on-hand, sales, and profit projection**	To enter additional information about the workbook content, as shown in Exhibit 8-1.
Close the Document Panel	Click the "X" in the top-right corner of the panel.
4 Update and close the workbook	To save these changes.

5 Display the Open dialog box

Point to **My quantity**

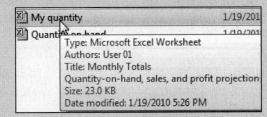

A ScreenTip appears with file information, including comments and some of the other information you added in the Document Panel. Note that the Company name is not included.

Click **Cancel**

To close the Open dialog box without opening the file.

Topic C: Protection

This topic covers the following Microsoft Office Specialist objectives for exam 77-888: Excel Expert 2010.

#	Objective
1.2	**Apply protection and sharing properties to workbooks and worksheets**
	1.2.1 Protect the current sheet
	1.2.2 Protect the workbook structure
	1.2.4 Require a password to open a workbook

Applying password protection to a worksheet

Explanation

By protecting a worksheet, you can prevent unauthorized users from modifying it. You can protect an entire worksheet or protect only a part of it, permitting users to alter the other parts. You can also protect workbooks by using digital signatures.

You might need to prevent the data in a worksheet from being altered accidentally or accessed by unauthorized users. You can use the Protect Sheet dialog box to password-protect a worksheet.

To password-protect a worksheet:

1 Click the Review tab.

2 In the Changes group, click Protect Sheet to open the Protect Sheet dialog box, shown in Exhibit 8-2.

3 Check the options you want.

4 Type a password and click OK. The Confirm Password dialog box appears.

5 In the "Reenter password to proceed" box, type the same password.

6 Click OK to close both the password confirmation box and the dialog box.

Before entering data into a password-protected sheet, you must unprotect it. To do so, click Unprotect Sheet in the Changes group; this opens the Unprotect Sheet dialog box. Enter the password and click OK.

Exhibit 8-2: The Protect Sheet dialog box

Do it!

C-1: Password-protecting a worksheet

The files for this activity are in Student Data folder **Unit 8\Topic C**.

Here's how	Here's why
1 Open Monthly totals and save it as **My monthly totals**	In the current topic folder.
2 Click the **Review** tab	If necessary.
3 In the Changes group, click **Protect Sheet**	
	To open the Protect Sheet dialog box, shown in Exhibit 8-2. The "Protect worksheet and contents of locked cells" option is checked by default. In the "Allow all users of this worksheet to" list, only "Select locked cells" and "Select unlocked cells" are checked.
In the "Password to unprotect sheet" box, enter **User01**	The entry in this field is masked by a row of dots to prevent it from being read by anyone else. This masking occurs in all fields in which you enter a password.
Click **OK**	To open the Confirm Password dialog box.
4 In the "Reenter password to proceed" box, enter **User01**	
Click **OK**	To confirm the password you entered. Both this box and the Protect Sheet dialog box close.
5 Enter a new value in B11	A message box states that the cell is protected, so you cannot enter a value or change the worksheet.
Click **OK**	To close the message box.
6 Click **Unprotect Sheet**	
	A dialog box prompts you for the password.
In the Password box, enter **User01**	
Click **OK**	
7 In B11, enter **1.5**	You can now enter a value in the worksheet.
8 Update the workbook	

Protecting parts of a worksheet

Explanation

When you password-protect an entire worksheet, all cells in that worksheet are locked by default. This means that users cannot change any of the cells. To permit users to change some specific cells, you must unlock those cells manually before protecting the rest of the worksheet. Users can then change data in only the unlocked cells. The rest of the worksheet remains protected. One typical application of this feature is to unlock the cells containing raw values to permit data entry, and lock the cells containing formulas.

To protect only a part of a worksheet:

1. Select the range of cells that you want users to be able to modify.
2. Right-click and choose Format Cells to open the Format Cells dialog box.
3. Click the Protection tab.
4. Clear the Locked checkbox and click OK.
5. Protect the worksheet. You don't necessarily need to use a password.

Do it!

C-2: Unlocking cells and protecting part of a worksheet

Here's how	Here's why
1 Select B7:B13	You'll keep these cells unlocked while protecting the rest of the worksheet.
2 Right-click and choose **Format Cells...**	To open the Format Cells dialog box.
3 Click the **Protection** tab	
Clear **Locked**	
Click **OK**	To close the dialog box and unlock the selected range of cells.
4 Protect the sheet without entering a password	(In the Changes group, click Protect Sheet.) You'll protect the sheet, but users will be able to modify the unlocked cells in the range B7:B13.
Click **OK**	Because you did not enter a password, any user can unprotect the worksheet by using the Unprotect Sheet dialog box.
5 In B11, enter **2.5**	You can enter the value in the unlocked cell.
6 In D10, enter a value	A message box appears, stating that the cell is protected, and as a result, you cannot enter a value or change the worksheet.
Click **OK**	
7 Click **Unprotect Sheet**	
Update the workbook	

Protecting a workbook

Explanation

To protect a workbook, click Protect Workbook in the Changes group on the Review tab. In the Protect Structure and Windows dialog box, you can protect a workbook's structure, windows, or both.

- Check Structure to protect the workbook's worksheets from being deleted, moved, hidden, unhidden, or renamed. In addition, new worksheets can't be inserted.
- Check Windows to ensure that the workbook's windows are the same size and position each time the workbook is opened.

To prevent other users from removing workbook protection, you can set a password. Then click OK.

Do it!

C-3: Protecting the workbook structure

Here's how	Here's why
1 Right-click the Sales Report worksheet	
Choose **Hide**	To hide the Sales Report sheet.
2 In the Changes group, click **Protect Workbook**	To open the Protect Structure and Windows dialog box.
3 Verify that **Structure** is checked	Protecting the workbook structure prevents users from inserting, deleting, moving, hiding, or renaming worksheets.
4 In the Password box, enter **password**	
Click **OK**	
5 Re-enter **password**	To confirm the password and proceed with protecting the workbook.
6 Unhide the Sales Report sheet	(Use Shift+click to select both sheet tabs, and right-click to display the shortcut menu.) The sheet commands, including Unhide, are not available.
7 Click **Protect Workbook**	The Unprotect Workbook dialog box opens.
Enter **password** and click **OK**	To unprotect the workbook.
8 Unhide the Sales Report sheet	When you right-click the sheet tabs, all of the commands are available.
Update and close the workbook	

Protecting worksheets by using digital signatures

Explanation

When you send worksheets or other documents over the Internet, there is a chance that someone might access and alter them. To protect your documents from unauthorized access, you can use digital signatures. A *digital signature* is an electronic security stamp that is used to authenticate files that are sent over the Internet. To use a digital signature, you need to install a *digital certificate*, which is an attachment that guarantees security for a file.

To obtain a digital certificate, you submit an application to a commercial certification authority, such as VeriSign Inc. You can go to the online Office Marketplace to see a list of third-party digital-signature service providers.

You can also obtain a digital certificate from your internal security administrator or from an Information Technology professional. It's also possible to create your own digital certificates, called *self-signed projects*. However, self-signed projects might not be legally valid because they are not sanctioned by any legal authority and can be authenticated only on the computers that were used to create the digital signatures.

When you receive a digital certificate, included are instructions on how to install it on your computer. After installing the certificate, you can use it to sign the files that you send over the Internet.

To add a digital signature:

1 Save the workbook.
2 Click the File tab and choose Info.
3 Click Protect Workbook and choose Add a Digital Signature to open the Signature dialog box. A message explaining the legal enforceability of digital signatures might appear. Click OK to close it.
4 Complete the "Purpose for signing this document" box and click Sign.

Do it!

C-4: Discussing digital signatures

Questions and answers
1 What is a digital signature?
2 Why do you need a digital signature?
3 What is a digital certificate?
4 If you create your own digital certificate, is it legally valid?

Topic D: Workgroup collaboration

This topic covers the following Microsoft Office Specialist objectives for exam 77-882: Excel 2010.

#	Objective
1.3	**Personalize the environment by using Backstage**
	1.3.1 Manipulate the Quick Access Toolbar
	1.3.4 Manipulate workbook properties (Document Panel)
	1.3.5 Manipulate workbook files and folders
	1.3.5.1 Manage versions

This topic covers the following Microsoft Office Specialist objectives for exam 77-888: Excel Expert 2010.

#	Objective
1.2	**Apply protection and sharing properties to workbooks and worksheets**
	1.2.3 Restrict permissions
1.3	**Maintain shared workbooks**
	1.3.1 Merge workbooks
	1.3.2 Set Track Changes options

Sharing workbooks

Explanation

Sharing a workbook makes it possible for several co-workers to collaborate on the same set of data. For example, several sales managers could enter their respective regional sales figures in the same workbook, eliminating the need to collect and consolidate the data manually.

To share a workbook:

1 Open the workbook that you want to share.
2 Click the Review tab.
3 In the Changes group, click Share Workbook to open the Share Workbook dialog box. Click the Editing tab.
4 Check "Allow changes by more than one user at the same time" and click OK.
5 Save the workbook in a location where other users can access it.

Modifying a shared workbook

To edit a shared workbook, open it from its network location. Then make changes in the workbook as usual.

When modifying a shared workbook, you won't be able to change the following elements: merged cells, conditional formats, data validation, charts, pictures, objects (including drawing objects), hyperlinks, scenarios, outlines, subtotals, data tables, PivotTable reports, workbook and worksheet protection, and macros.

Do it!

D-1:   Sharing a workbook

The files for this activity are in Student Data folder **Unit 8\Topic D**.

Here's how	Here's why
1 Open Sales	
Save the workbook as **My sales**	In the current topic folder.
Click the **Review** tab	If necessary.
2 In the Changes group, click **Share Workbook**	 To open the Share Workbook dialog box. By default, the Editing tab is active.
3 Check **Allow changes by more than one user at the same time**	
Click **OK**	A message box appears, warning you that this action will save the workbook.
Click **OK**	My sales [Shared] – Microsoft Excel The name of the workbook changes to "My sales [Shared]."

Merging workbooks

Explanation

You might need to share a workbook among users who cannot access the same file simultaneously. You can do this by distributing copies of the shared workbook, permitting users to change their copies, and then merging those copies into a single workbook. To begin, share the workbook as described previously. Then make copies of the workbook and distribute them to the users.

You can control how a workbook is shared by using the Advanced tab in the Share Workbook dialog box, shown in Exhibit 8-3. For example, under Update changes, you can select "When file is saved" to see the changes made by other users each time you save the workbook. You can also set the interval at which changes will automatically be shown.

After the users have changed their copies of the workbook, you can merge the copies into a single workbook. To merge workbooks:

1   Click the File tab and choose Options to open the Excel Options dialog box.
2   Select Quick Access Toolbar, and add the Compare and Merge Workbooks command to the toolbar.
3   On the Quick Access toolbar, click the Compare and Merge Workbooks button to open the Select Files to Merge Into Current Workbook dialog box.
4   Select the copies of the workbook that contain changes you want to merge.
5   Click OK.

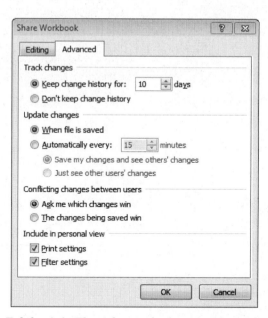

Exhibit 8-3: The Advanced tab in the Share Workbook dialog box

Do it!

D-2: Merging workbooks

The files for this activity are in Student Data folder **Unit 8\Topic D**.

Here's how	Here's why
1 Open the Excel Options dialog box	(Click the File tab and choose Options.) You'll make a merging command available by adding it to the Quick Access toolbar.
In the category list, select **Quick Access Toolbar**	To display the Customize the Quick Access Toolbar page.
Under Customize Quick Access toolbar, verify that **For all documents (default)** is selected	Customize Quick Access Toolbar: ⓘ For all documents (default) ▼ You'll make these changes effective for all workbooks, not just the one that's open.
2 Under "Choose commands from," select **All commands**	To display all available commands.
Select **Compare and Merge Workbooks...**	(Scroll down.) Commands are listed in alphabetical order.
Click **Add**	To add the Compare and Merge Workbooks command to the Quick Access toolbar.
Click **OK**	To save the changes and close the Excel Options dialog box.
3 Open the Share Workbook dialog box	In the Changes group, click Share Workbook.
Click the **Advanced** tab	Under Track changes, "Keep change history for" is selected. You'll maintain a history of changes made by various users.
Under Track changes, edit the days box to read **10**	(As shown in Exhibit 8-3.) This setting permits users to track the change history for 10 days.
Click **OK**	
4 Click the Sales report worksheet	If necessary.
Update the workbook	
5 Save the workbook as **Copy of my sales**	You'll merge this workbook with another one.
6 Select A4:E4	You'll change the format of the data, and see the changes being applied to the workbook My sales.
Right-click the selection	The Mini toolbar appears.

7	On the Mini toolbar, click the Fill Color arrow, as shown	
		To display the Fill Color gallery.
	Apply light blue shading to the selection	
8	Apply light green shading to A5:A14	Right-click, and select a color by using the Fill Color button on the Mini toolbar.
9	Apply another color of shading to A15:E15	
	Deselect the range	
	Update and close the workbook	
10	Open My sales and save it as **Copy 2 of my sales**	You'll consolidate the changes by merging the two copies of the workbook with the original workbook.
11	Verify that Sales report is the active worksheet	
	In B5, enter **840**	
	Update and close the workbook	
12	Open My sales	
13	On the Quick Access toolbar, click ⊙	(The Compare and Merge Workbooks icon.) You'll update the current workbook with the changes you made in "Copy of my sales" and "Copy 2 of my sales." The Select Files to Merge Into Current Workbook dialog box opens.
	Select **Copy of my sales**	In the current topic folder.
	Press ⌈CTRL⌉ and select **Copy 2 of my sales**	
	Click **OK**	
14	Observe the Sales report sheet	It reflects the changes you applied in "Copy of my sales." The ranges have the new shading, and the value in B5 is now $840.
15	Update the workbook	

Tracking changes

Explanation

You can use the Track Changes feature to examine the changes made in a workbook. You can identify who made changes, when they were made, what the original values were, and what the new values are. If your workbook is not shared, Excel automatically makes the workbook shared when you turn on the Track Changes feature.

To highlight changes:

1 Click the Review tab.

2 In the Changes group, click Track Changes and choose Highlight Changes to open the Highlight Changes dialog box, shown in Exhibit 8-4.

3 If the workbook is not shared, check "Track changes while editing." If the workbook is shared, this option will be checked by default.

4 Specify how you want the changes to be tracked:

- To view changes based on when they were made—for example, after a specific date—check When and select the desired setting from the list.

- To view the changes made by a specific user, check Who and select Everyone or Everyone but Me from the list.

- To view the changes made in a specific range, check Where and enter the range.

5 Click OK.

Exhibit 8-4: The Highlight Changes dialog box

To review workbook changes and accept or reject them:

1 Click the Review tab.

2 In the Changes group, click Track Changes and choose Accept/Reject Changes. You'll be prompted to save the workbook.

3 Click OK to save the workbook. The Select Changes to Accept or Reject dialog box appears.

4 If you want to view changes based on when they were made, check When and select a time period.

5 Click OK to open the Accept or Reject Changes dialog box. A cell that contains a changed value will be highlighted. The dialog box displays information about each change, including the name of the person who made the change, the date and time it was made, and other changes that will occur if you accept or reject the suggested change. You can scroll down to see the rest of the contents.

6 Click Accept to accept the change, or click Reject to restore the original value. The next cell with a changed value will be highlighted.

Do it!   **D-3:   Tracking changes in a workbook**

Here's how	Here's why
1 Click the **Profit projection** sheet	
2 In B7, enter **60000**	This is the new total sales value for Qtr 1.
3 Click the **Review** tab	If necessary.
In the Changes group, click **Track Changes** and choose **Highlight Changes...**	To open the Highlight Changes dialog box, shown in Exhibit 8-4. By default, "Since I last saved" is entered in the When box, and "Everyone" is entered in the Who box.
Click **OK**	
4 Point to B7	A comment appears, stating that the value in B7 has changed from $50,000.00 to $60,000.00. The comment includes the name of the user who made the change and the date and time it was made.
5 Click **Track Changes** and choose **Accept/Reject Changes**	(In the Changes group.) A message box appears, stating that the workbook will be saved.
Click **OK**	

Select Changes to Accept or Reject

Which changes

☑ When: Not yet reviewed
☐ Who: Everyone
☐ Where:

To open the Select Changes to Accept or Reject dialog box. By default, When is checked.

Click **OK**	

Accept or Reject Changes

Change 1 of 2 made to this document:

User 01, 1/19/2010 8:08 PM:

Changed cell B5 from '$534.00 ' to '$840.00 '.

Accept   Reject   Accept All   Reject All   Close

To open the Accept or Reject Changes dialog box, which shows the original and changed values for B5.

6 Click **Accept**	To accept the change. The dialog box now shows the original and changed values for B7.
Click **Accept**	To accept the next change.
7 Update the workbook	

Preparing workbooks for distribution

Explanation

Before sharing a workbook via e-mail, print, or the Web, you might want to be sure that any personal or hidden information contained in the workbook is removed. Hidden and personal details in a workbook could reveal information about you or your organization that you want to keep private.

Some types of hidden or personal information that might be found in a workbook include:

- Hidden rows, columns, or worksheets
- Document properties, such as the author, or workbook comments
- Cell comments and revision marks from tracked changes

To help you find and remove hidden or private information in a workbook, Excel provides the Document Inspector, shown in Exhibit 8-5.

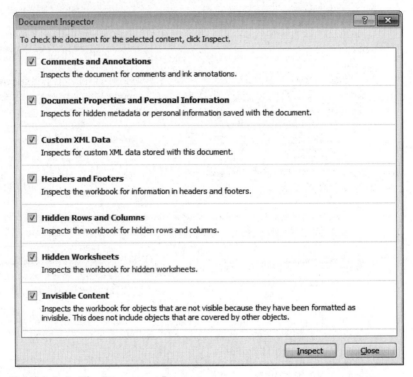

Exhibit 8-5: The Document Inspector

Note: Before using the Document Inspector, save a copy of the file you want to examine, and stop sharing the workbook. The Document Inspector might remove data that isn't possible to restore later, and it cannot remove data from a shared workbook.

To use the Document Inspector:

1 Click the File tab and display the Info page.
2 Click Check for Issues and choose Inspect Document to open the Document Inspector.
3 Check the items you want the Document Inspector to search for.
4 Click Inspect.
5 If you want to remove the hidden or private content found, click Remove All.
6 Click Close.

Do it!

D-4:   Using the Document Inspector

The files for this activity are in Student Data folder **Unit 8\Topic D**.

Here's how	Here's why
1 Save the workbook as **Copy 3 of my sales**	Even though you're making a copy of My sales, the copy is still shared. You have to stop sharing the workbook before using the Document Inspector.
2 In the Changes group, click **Share Workbook**	To open the Share Workbook dialog box.
On the Editing tab, clear **Allow changes by more than one user at the same time**	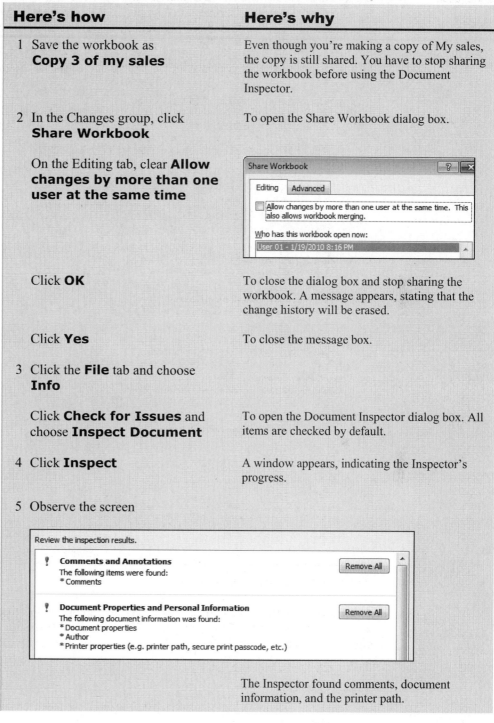
Click **OK**	To close the dialog box and stop sharing the workbook. A message appears, stating that the change history will be erased.
Click **Yes**	To close the message box.
3 Click the **File** tab and choose **Info**	
Click **Check for Issues** and choose **Inspect Document**	To open the Document Inspector dialog box. All items are checked by default.
4 Click **Inspect**	A window appears, indicating the Inspector's progress.
5 Observe the screen	
	The Inspector found comments, document information, and the printer path.

6	To the right of Comments and Annotations, click **Remove All**	To remove all comments from the workbook.
	Remove the document properties and personal information found	Click Remove All.
	Click **Close**	To close the Document Inspector.
7	Update the workbook	

Finalizing workbooks

When you have finished making changes and removing private data from a workbook, you can use the Mark as Final command to mark the workbook as read-only and prevent any further changes in it.

To mark a workbook as final, click the File tab and display the Info page. Click Protect Workbook and choose Mark as Final. A message box appears, stating that the workbook will be marked as final and then saved. Click OK. You will then see a message box with information about final documents, as shown in Exhibit 8-6.

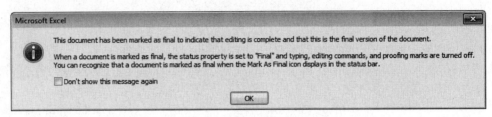

Exhibit 8-6: The message box that appears after you mark a workbook as final

Do it!

D-5: Marking a workbook as final

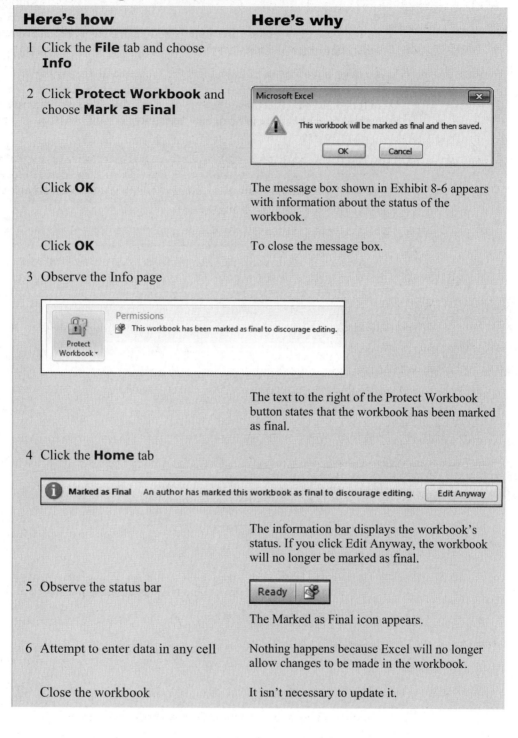

Here's how	Here's why
1 Click the **File** tab and choose **Info**	
2 Click **Protect Workbook** and choose **Mark as Final**	
Click **OK**	The message box shown in Exhibit 8-6 appears with information about the status of the workbook.
Click **OK**	To close the message box.
3 Observe the Info page	
	The text to the right of the Protect Workbook button states that the workbook has been marked as final.
4 Click the **Home** tab	
	The information bar displays the workbook's status. If you click Edit Anyway, the workbook will no longer be marked as final.
5 Observe the status bar	
	The Marked as Final icon appears.
6 Attempt to enter data in any cell	Nothing happens because Excel will no longer allow changes to be made in the workbook.
Close the workbook	It isn't necessary to update it.

Unit summary: Documenting and auditing

Topic A   In this topic, you used the Formula Auditing group to **trace precedent** and **dependent cells** and to view the relationships between formulas in a worksheet. You learned that a precedent cell provides a value to another cell, and a dependent cell depends on another cell for a value. You also **traced errors**.

Topic B   In this topic, you added **comments** to cells and changed how they are displayed. You changed the comment indicator settings. Finally, you used the Document Panel to add, edit, and delete comments for a workbook.

Topic C   In this topic, you **password-protected** a worksheet to prevent unauthorized users from changing it. You also protected only a part of a worksheet and unlocked cells that you want users to be able to modify. Next, you protected the **workbook structure**. Finally, you learned about **digital signatures**.

Topic D   In this topic, you **shared** workbooks and **merged** copies of shared workbooks that various users had changed. You learned that sharing a workbook permits multiple users to work on it at the same time. You also **tracked changes** and accepted or rejected the tracked changes. Finally, you used the **Document Inspector** to find and remove private data before distributing a workbook, and you marked a workbook as final.

Independent practice activity

In this activity, you'll add a comment to a cell and trace errors, precedent cells, and dependent cells. Then you'll unlock a range and protect the rest of the worksheet. Next, you'll share the workbook, merge changes from several workbooks, and track changes.

The files for this activity are in Student Data folder **Unit 8\Unit summary**.

1 Open Practice profits and save it as **My practice profits**.

2 In B5, add this comment: **Constantly increasing fixed costs kept the profit percentage low.**

3 Trace the cells causing the error value in F7.

4 Trace the precedent and dependent cells for D5.

5 Compare your result with Exhibit 8-7.

6 Remove all arrows.

7 Unlock B4:C9; then protect the worksheet, using **password** as a password.

8 Unprotect the worksheet.

9 Update the workbook.

10 Share the workbook, allowing changes by more than one user at a time.

11 Save the workbook as **Copy of my practice profits**. Then, in the Bonus sales analysis sheet, apply shading to A6:E6, and a different color shading to A8:E22. When you're done, update the workbook and close it.

12 Open My practice profits.

13 Merge My practice profits with Copy of my practice profits, and observe the changes in the Bonus sales analysis sheet.

14 In the Bonus sales report sheet, in A3, enter **Name**. In E5, enter **5000**. Track the changes you made. Restore the original value in A3. Accept the change in E5.

15 Stop sharing the workbook.

16 Run the Document Inspector to search for inappropriate or private data. Remove all instances found.

17 Mark the workbook as final.

18 Close the workbook.

	A	B	C	D	E	F
1						
2			**Regional Profits**			
3	Region	Fixed cost	Variable cost	Total cost	Total revenue	%Profit
4	North	60000	55000	115000	135000	15%
5	South	80000	75000	155000	160000	3%
6	East	90000	80000	170000	182000	7%
7	Central	107500	88000	195500		#DIV/0!
8	West	109000	90000	199000	225000	12%
9	HQ	110000	96000	206000	236000	13%
10						

Exhibit 8-7: The worksheet after Step 5

Review questions

1 What are precedent and dependent cells? How can you identify them in a worksheet?

2 When you click the Trace Error button, you'll see red and/or blue tracer arrows pointing from the cell containing the error to other cells. What do the red and blue arrows mean?

3 List the steps you would use to password-protect a worksheet.

4 If you choose to protect a workbook's structure, what kinds of changes are affected?

5 What is a digital signature?

6 When should you use the Document Inspector?

Unit 9

Templates and settings

Unit time: 35 minutes

Complete this unit, and you'll know how to:

A Change Excel's default application settings.

B Use Excel's built-in templates to create invoices.

C Create and manage custom templates.

Topic A: Changing application settings

This topic covers the following Microsoft Office Specialist objectives for exam 77-882: Excel 2010.

#	Objective
1.3	**Personalize the environment by using Backstage**
	1.3.2 Customize the Ribbon
	1.3.2.1 Tabs
	1.3.2.2 Groups
	1.3.3 Manipulate Excel default settings (Excel Options)
	1.3.5 Manipulate workbook files and folders
	1.3.5.2 AutoSave

This topic covers the following Microsoft Office Specialist objectives for exam 77-888: Excel Expert 2010.

#	Objective
1.1	**Apply workbook settings, properties, and data options**
	1.1.1 Set advanced properties

The Excel Options dialog box

Explanation

The Excel Options dialog box contains settings for specifying how Excel starts and operates. Often, though, the default settings don't provide you with the environment that's best for your working habits. For example, you might want to change the format in which data appears, or change the number of worksheets in a new workbook. You might want to personalize your copy of Excel or save your worksheets in a different location. The Excel Options dialog box, shown in Exhibit 9-1, can be used to change these and other settings.

To open the Excel Options dialog box, click the File tab and choose Options. The Excel Options dialog box contains the following pages:

Page	Description
General	Basic options for setting application defaults.
Formulas	Options that set defaults for how formulas are calculated in a worksheet.
Proofing	Options to configure the spelling checker and other correction features.
Save	Options related to saving working files and AutoRecover settings.
Language	Options related to languages used while editing and when accessing Help.
Advanced	Advanced options for setting application defaults, including editing and display options.

Page	Description
Customize Ribbon	Options for adding frequently used commands to the Ribbon, as well as adding commands that are not located on one of the standard tabs.
Quick Access Toolbar	Options for adding frequently used commands to the Quick Access Toolbar.
Add-ins	Options for managing plug-ins and other extensions that can be developed for Excel.
Trust Center	Options related to privacy and computer security.

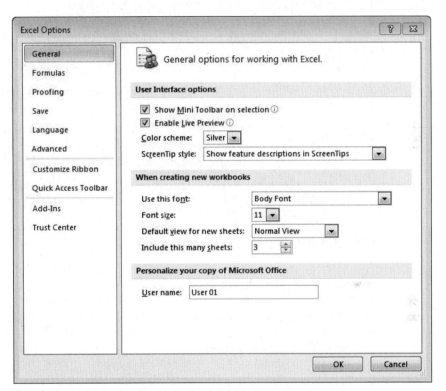

Exhibit 9-1: The General page in the Excel Options dialog box

Do it!   **A-1:**   **Changing application settings**

Here's how	Here's why
1 Create a new, blank workbook	Press Ctrl+N.
2 Click the **File** tab	The File tab contains file management commands, such as Save, Save As, Open, and Close, as well as general application settings.
Choose **Options**	To open the Excel Options dialog box. As shown in Exhibit 9-1, the General page is active. It contains basic display and personalization options.
3 Under "Personalize your copy of Microsoft Office," observe the User name box	Your instructor entered a user name for you earlier. You'll change it to your own name.
In the User name box, enter your name	

Personalize your copy of Microsoft Office

User name: Laurie Perry

4 Select **Save**	
Under "Save workbooks," observe the Save AutoRecover information	To prevent you from losing data, Excel will automatically save the workbook every 10 minutes. In addition, the last autosaved version will be kept even if you close the workbook before saving it.
Edit the Save AutoRecover interval to **15** minutes	

☑ Save AutoRecover information every   15   ⬍   minutes

☑ Keep the last autosaved version if I close without saving

5 Select **Advanced**	This page includes display and editing settings.
Scroll down and observe the various options	Some of the settings can be applied to a specific worksheet or to the entire workbook.
Under General, click **Edit Custom Lists**	The Custom Lists dialog box appears. You'll create a custom list that can be used in Outlander Spices workbooks.

6 In the List entries box, enter
**North, South, East,
Central, West**

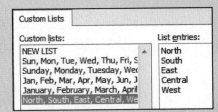

(Enter the commas, along with the region names.) Many of Outlander Spices' sales worksheets are organized by sales regions. A predefined list of regions would be useful when you're creating worksheets.

Click **Add**

The list of sales regions joins the other sequences in the Custom lists box. In the List entries box, each entry appears on a separate line.

7 Click **OK**

To close the Custom Lists dialog box and return to the Excel Options dialog box.

Customizing the Ribbon

Explanation

A new feature in Excel 2010 is the ability to customize the Ribbon tabs. You can add commands to and remove them from the standard tabs, change the order of the tabs, and add or remove tabs.

To create a custom tab on the Ribbon:

1 Click the File tab and choose Options to open the Excel Options dialog box.
2 Select Customize Ribbon to display the Customize Ribbon page, shown in Exhibit 9-2.
3 Click the New Tab button (near the lower-right corner of the dialog box).
4 Click the Move Up and Move Down arrows to rearrange the tabs.
5 Use the Rename button to change the name of the new tab and the new group.
6 In the list of commands on the left, select the command you want to add to the new custom tab. (If you are searching for a command not currently on the Ribbon, you will first need to display the "Choose commands from" list and select Commands Not in the Ribbon.)
7 Click Add to add the command to the tab.
8 Click OK to close the Excel Options dialog box and save your changes.

To remove a Ribbon tab, select the tab to be removed from the Customize the Ribbon list, and click Remove.

To return the Ribbon to its original state, click Reset and choose Reset all customizations.

Exhibit 9-2: The Customize Ribbon page

Do it!

A-2:   Customizing the Ribbon

The files for this activity are in Student Data folder **Unit 9\Topic A**.

Here's how	Here's why
1 In the Excel Options dialog box, select **Customize Ribbon**	You can use this page to add commands that are not on one of the standard Ribbon tabs.
Click **New Tab**	To add a new tab in the Customize the Ribbon list box.
2 Select the new tab	☐ ☑ New Tab (Custom) New Group (Custom)
Click [▼] repeatedly	To move the new tab near the bottom of the list, just above Background Removal.
3 With the new tab selected, click **Rename**	To open the Rename dialog box.
In the Display name box, enter your name	To rename the new Ribbon tab "*Your name* (Custom)."
4 From the "Choose commands from" list, select **Commands Not in the Ribbon**	You can scroll down to see a lengthy list of commands not currently on the Ribbon.
Select **Calculator**	In the list box.
Select the new group on your custom tab	To add the Calculator command to your new tab.
Click **Add**	The Calculator command is added to the new group as Custom. You'll rename the button to provide a more accurate description.

5 Select the new **Custom** command	☐ ☑ Laurie (Custom)
	     ☐ New Group (Custom)
	          ▦ Custom

	Currently, the new button's name is Custom. You'll rename the button.
Click **Rename**	
In the Display name box, enter **Calculator**	Because the calculator icon is already attached to the button, you do not need to select an icon at this time.
Click **OK**	To close the Rename dialog box.

6	Click **OK**	To close the Excel Options dialog box and apply your changes.
	Click the new tab	The new tab appears, with your name on it, as the last tab. The new group contains the Calculator button. You can rename the group and continue to customize this Ribbon tab.
7	Close the blank worksheet	If prompted, don't save changes.

Topic B: Using built-in templates

Explanation

You can use a template to create multiple workbooks that have the same settings. A *template* is a workbook with predefined settings on which you can base new workbooks. Templates can contain labels and other data, formatting, styles, and functionality such as formulas.

Using Excel templates

If you have an Internet connection, you have access to Office.com, from which you can download hundreds of templates for business, education, and personal use. You can see these templates by clicking the File tab and choosing New. As shown in Exhibit 9-3, the templates are divided into local and online groups. The local templates reside on your computer and appear under the Home banner. The online templates are listed under the Office.com Templates banner. The right-side pane displays a preview of the selected template.

To create a worksheet using the Blank workbook template, selected in Exhibit 9-3, you can either click the Create button under the template preview or double-click the template itself. If the selected template is an online template, you can double-click it or click the Download button to download it from Office.com.

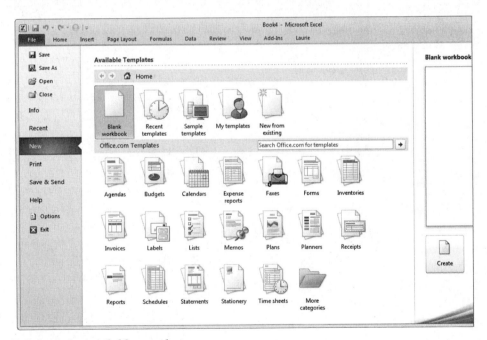

Exhibit 9-3: Available templates

Creating a workbook from a template

You can use one of the Sales invoice templates to create invoices, like the example shown in Exhibit 9-4. In a sales invoice, you can include company details (such as name and address), customer details, order details, and payment details.

To use the "Sales invoice with stock number" template:

1   Click the File tab and choose New.

2   In the templates list, under Office.com Templates, click Invoices.

3   Find the "Sales invoice with stock number" template.

4   Double-click the template to download and open it. Or you can click the Download button under the template preview.

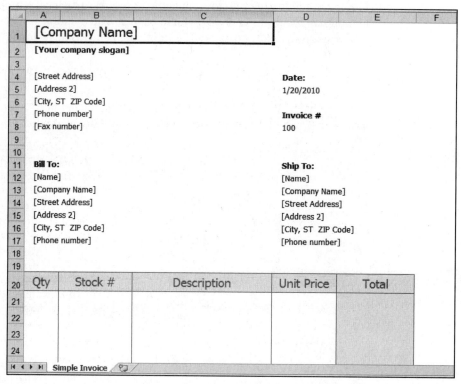

Exhibit 9-4: A portion of the "Sales invoice with stock number" template

Do it!

B-1: Using a downloaded template

Here's how	Here's why
1 Click the **File** tab and choose **New**	To display the Available Templates page.
Observe the available templates	The templates are divided into local and Office.com templates. By default, the Blank Workbook template is selected, and a preview (thumbnail) of it is displayed on the right side of the page. You can click the Create button to create a new workbook from this template.
2 In the Search Office.com for templates box, enter **Sales Invoice**	You'll search for a suitable template for a sales invoice.
Observe the template thumbnails	You can see what each template looks like.
3 Select **Sales invoice with stock number**	For online templates, the Create button becomes a Download button.
Click **Download**	The Microsoft Office Genuine Advantage message box appears briefly. Microsoft is verifying that you have a legitimate copy of the software.
Click **Continue**	To download the template. When the template finishes downloading, the title bar of the new workbook displays "Sales invoice with stock number1," indicating that this is a workbook based on that template.
4 Open the Save As dialog box	
Navigate to the current topic folder	C:\Student Data\Unit 9\Topic B.
Edit the File name box to read **My invoice**	
Click **Save**	To save the workbook with the new name.

5	Click **Company Name**	In the upper-left corner of the worksheet.

Enter the company details, as shown

Outlander Spices

adding spice to your life

61 Rock Creek Drive
Attn: Fulfillment Center
Portland, OR 97201
735-555-0948
735-555-0950

6 Enter the Bill To details, as shown

Bill To:
Adam Hayward
Spice of Life, Inc.
7 Ulster Street
[Address 2]
Denver, CO 80237
720-555-1070

7 Enter the indicated Qty, Description, and Unit Price details

Qty	Stock #	Description	Unit Price	Total
25	1701	Cassia	$750.00	$18,750.
45	1719	Cilantro Flakes	$800.00	$36,000.

The Total value for each product is calculated automatically when you enter the Qty and Unit Price. The Subtotal and Total values for the entire invoice are also calculated automatically.

8 Select A37

Observe the formula bar

fx ="Make all checks payable to "&A1

This cell refers to the company name you entered.

9 Edit A39 to read as shown

Kim Leong, 735-555-0955, kleong@outlanderspices.com

10 Update and close the workbook

Topic C: Creating and managing templates

This topic covers the following Microsoft Office Specialist objectives for exam 77-888: Excel Expert 2010.

#	Objective
1.2	**Apply workbook settings, properties, and data options**
	1.1.1 Set advanced properties
	1.1.2 Save a workbook as a template

Explanation

If the templates provided in Excel do not contain all the functionality you need, you can create your own templates—either from scratch or by modifying one of the Microsoft templates. You can use custom templates to create and maintain multiple workbooks with the same formatting, styles, content, and functionality.

Custom templates

To create a template:

1   Open or create the workbook on which you want to base the template.
2   Open the Save As dialog box.
3   From the Save as type list, select Excel Template, as shown in Exhibit 9-5.
4   In the File name box, enter a name for the template. The default name is the active workbook.
5   Click Save.

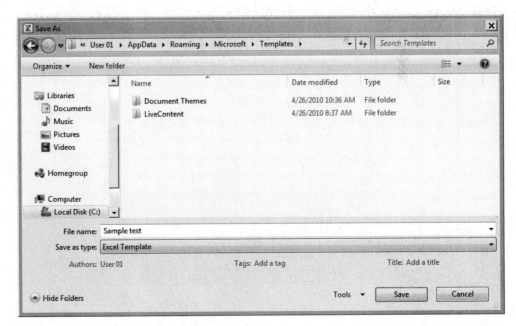

Exhibit 9-5: Saving a workbook as a template

Do it!

C-1: Creating a template

The files for this activity are in Student Data folder **Unit 9\Topic C**.

Here's how	Here's why
1 Open Sample test	You'll use this workbook as the basis for a new template. This workbook contains two linked worksheets: Observations and Results.
2 Open the Save As dialog box	
From the Save as type list, select **Excel Template**	To create a template file based on this workbook. The Save in box contains "Templates," indicating that Excel saves templates in the Templates folder by default. The File name box contains "Sample test," indicating that Excel saves the template with the name of the workbook on which it's based.
Click **Save**	To create the Sample test template.
3 Close the template	
4 Display the Available Templates page	You'll create a workbook based on the Sample test template.
Under Home, click **My templates**	 My templates To open the New dialog box.
Select **Sample test**	 Your newly created template appears on the Personal Templates tab.
Click **OK**	The workbook opens as Sample Test1.
5 Save the file as an Excel Workbook with the file name **My test**	In Student Data folder Unit 9\Topic C.

6 Under Sample Details, enter the indicated information

Sample Details	
Product	Anise seed
Sample Code	S001
Test Type	T005
Sample Date	6/16/2010

7 Click the **Results** sheet

Formulas in the Results worksheet automatically carry over data from the Observations worksheet.

8 Update and close the workbook

Modifying templates

Explanation

You might sometimes need to modify custom templates. In Windows 7, Excel templates are stored in C:\Users*user_name*\AppData\Roaming\Microsoft\Templates.

The Recent Workbooks list provides an easy way to navigate to recently used files. The icons to the left of the file names indicate the file type: workbook, template, or workspace. To open a file from this list, click the File tab, choose Recent, and click the desired file.

To modify a template:

1 Display the Open dialog box.
2 Navigate to the template folder, select the template to be modified, and click Open.
3 Make your changes and update the template.

Do it!

C-2: Modifying a template

Here's how	Here's why
1 Click the **File** tab and choose **Recent**	Using the Recent Workbooks list is the easiest way to reopen the Sample test template because you recently worked on it.
Select **Sample test**, as shown	

	To open the Sample test template from C:\Users*user_name*\AppData\Roaming\Microsoft\Templates.
2 In A11, enter **Tested By**	
3 Copy the contents of A11	
Click the **Results** sheet	
Select A11 and click **Paste**	
4 Click the **Observations** sheet	To ensure that this is the active worksheet when the template is saved.
5 Update and close the template	
6 Create a workbook based on the Sample test template	(On the File tab, click New. Click My Templates and double-click Sample test.) You can see the changes you made in the template.
7 Close the workbook	You need not save changes.

Using an alternate template location

Explanation

When you save a workbook as a template in Windows 7, by default the template is saved in the C:\Users*user_name*\AppData\Roaming\Microsoft\Templates folder. If you have a template stored in a location other than this default folder, it will not automatically appear on the Available Templates page.

To specify an alternate template location and have Excel open those templates automatically:

1   Open the Excel Options dialog box.

2   In the category list, select Advanced.

3   Under General, in the "At startup, open all files in" box, type the path to the folder containing the template files.

4   Click OK.

Do it!   **C-3:   Specifying an alternate template location**

Here's how	Here's why
1 Open the Excel Options dialog box	
In the category list, select **Advanced**	
Under General, in the "At startup, open all files" box, enter the path for the Alternate Template folder	Depending on your installation, this might be C:\Users*user_name*\Desktop\Student Data\Unit 9\Topic C\Alternate Template.
Click **OK**	To close the Excel Options dialog box.
2 Close any open workbooks and close Excel	The new setting won't take effect until you restart Excel.
3 Restart Excel	
Close the blank workbook	
4 Click the **File** tab and choose **New**	
5 Select **My templates**	
	The New dialog box opens, with the Alt template in the Alternate Template folder selected.
6 Click **Cancel**	To close the New dialog box and return to the Available Templates page.
7 Open the Excel Options dialog box	
Select **Advanced**	If necessary.
Delete the path for alternate templates	Under General, in the "At startup, open all files in" box.
Click **OK**	The alternate template location has been removed.

Unit summary: Templates and settings

Topic A   In this topic, you learned about Excel's **application settings**. You changed defaults that control the way Excel operates and displays data. You also **customized the Ribbon** by creating a tab and adding a command to it.

Topic B   In this topic, you learned about **templates**, which can be used as a basis to create multiple workbooks. You also downloaded and used a template from Office.com.

Topic C   In this topic, you created **custom templates** that contain your preferred formatting, styles, content, and functionality. You also modified a custom template and specified an alternate location for template files.

Independent practice activity

In this activity, you'll add a command to the Quick Access toolbar. You'll also download and save a template, and use it to create an invoice for a customer.

The files for this activity are in Student Data folder **Unit 9\Unit summary**.

1 Add the Open command to the Quick Access toolbar.

2 Create a workbook based on the "Sales invoice with stock number" template. (*Hint:* On the Available Templates page, click My Templates.) Save the workbook as **My spice invoice** in the current Unit Summary folder.

3 Customize the form to include company details, such as name and address.

4 Save the workbook as a template named **My OS invoice**.

5 Close the template.

6 Create a workbook based on the My OS invoice template, and save it in the Unit Summary folder with the default file name (My OS invoice1).

7 In the My OS invoice1 worksheet, enter customer details as shown in Exhibit 9-6.

8 Update and close the workbook.

Bill To:			**Ship To:**	
David Skipton			David Skipton	
The Spice House			The Spice House	
411 Princeton Ave			411 Princeton Ave	
[Address 2]			[Address 2]	
Astoria, OR 97103			Astoria, OR 97103	
563-555-0000			563-555-0000	

Qty	Stock #	Description	Unit Price	Total
20	1735	Cinnamon	$650.00	**$13,000.00**
15	1761	Nutmeg	$300.00	**$4,500.00**
25	1745	Bay leaf	$400.00	**$10,000.00**

Exhibit 9-6: The customer details for Step 7

Review questions

1 What worksheet elements can be contained in a template?

2 Where can you view Excel's built-in templates?

3 List the steps you would use to modify a custom template.

4 When you save a workbook as a template on a Windows 7 computer, in what folder is it saved by default?

5 True or false? If a template is stored in a location other than the default folder, it will not automatically appear on the Available Templates page.

Unit 10

PivotTables and PivotCharts

Unit time: 50 minutes

Complete this unit, and you'll know how to:

A Use the PivotTable command to create a PivotTable for analyzing and comparing large amounts of data.

B Change PivotTable views by moving fields and hiding and showing details.

C Improve the appearance of a PivotTable by applying a style and changing its field settings.

D Create a PivotChart to graphically display data from a PivotTable.

Topic A: Working with PivotTables

This topic covers the following Microsoft Office Specialist objectives for exam 77-888: Excel Expert 2010.

#	Objective
3.3	**Apply and manipulate PivotTables**
	3.3.1 Manipulate PivotTable data
	3.3.2 Use the slicer to filter and segment your PivotTable data in multiple layers
3.5	**Demonstrate how to use the slicer**
	3.5.1 Choose data sets from external data connection

Examining PivotTables

Explanation

By analyzing data, you can make more informed decisions. Excel provides the PivotTable feature to help you examine data. A *PivotTable* is an interactive table that summarizes, organizes, and compares large amounts of data in a worksheet. You can rotate the rows and columns in a PivotTable to obtain different views of the same data. You can use a PivotTable to analyze data in an Excel workbook or data from an external database, such as Microsoft Access or SQL Server.

The data on which a PivotTable is based is called the *source data*. Each column represents a *field*, or category of information, which you can assign to different parts of the PivotTable to determine how the data is arranged. You can add four types of fields, shown in Exhibit 10-1 and explained in the following table:

Field	Description
Report Filter	Filters the summarized data in the PivotTable. If you select an item in the report filter, the view of the PivotTable changes to display only the summarized data associated with that item. For example, if Region is a report filter, you can display the summarized data for the North region, the West region, or all regions.
Row Labels	Displays the items in a field as row labels. For example, in Exhibit 10-1, the row labels are values in the Quarter field, which means that the table shows one row for each quarter.
Column Labels	Displays the items in a field as column labels. For example, in Exhibit 10-1, the column labels are values in the Product field, which means that the table shows one column for each product.
Σ Values	Contains the summarized data. These fields usually contain numeric data, such as sales and inventory figures. The area where the data itself appears is called the *data area*.

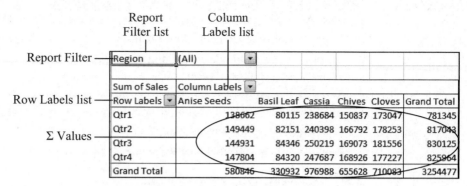

Exhibit 10-1: A sample PivotTable

The PivotTable command

You use the PivotTable command to create a PivotTable. Here's how:

1   Select any cell in a data range that includes a heading for each column in the top row.

2   Click the Insert tab.

3   In the Tables group, click the PivotTable button to open the Create PivotTable dialog box, shown in Exhibit 10-2. (Or click the PivotTable button's arrow and choose PivotTable.)

4   In the Table/Range box, select the range that contains the data you want to use in the PivotTable.

5   Select a location for the PivotTable. You can place the PivotTable in a new or existing worksheet.

6   Click OK.

When you insert or work with PivotTables, Excel displays the PivotTable Tools, adding Options and Design tabs to the Ribbon.

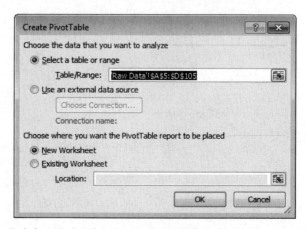

Exhibit 10-2: The Create PivotTable dialog box

Using an external data source

You can use an external data source as the data for the PivotTable. To do so:

1 In an empty worksheet, click the Insert tab and click the PivotTables button.

2 In the Create PivotTables dialog box, select "Use an external data source" and click Choose Connection.

3 From the list of connections, select the desired connection, such as an Access database. If the connection you want is not showing, click Browse for More.

4 Click Open. The selected data source appears as the Connection name.

5 Click OK to continue creating the PivotTable.

Do it!

A-1: Creating a PivotTable

The files for this activity are in Student Data folder **Unit 10\Topic A**.

Here's how	Here's why
1 Open Sales analysis	The Raw Data worksheet contains the sales details for several products. You'll use the data in this worksheet to create a PivotTable.
2 Save the workbook as **My sales analysis**	In the current topic folder.
3 Select any cell in the range A5:D105	You'll create a PivotTable based on this range. If you select a cell within the range of the source data, you won't have to specify the range later.
4 Click the **Insert** tab	
5 In the Tables group, click	(The top half of the PivotTable button.) To open the Create PivotTable dialog box. It prompts you to select the location of the data you want to analyze. You can use an external data source or an Excel worksheet. The default is the range that Excel automatically determines from the selected cell, as shown in Exhibit 10-2.
	You can create the PivotTable in a new or existing worksheet. The default selection is New Worksheet.
Click **OK**	A new worksheet, Sheet1, is added to the workbook. This worksheet displays the layout of the PivotTable. The PivotTable Field List pane appears, and the PivotTable Tools	Options and Design tabs appear on the Ribbon.
6 Edit the Sheet1 tab name to read **PivotTable**	Double-click the name, type the new one, and press Enter.
7 Update the workbook	

Adding fields

Explanation

You can add fields to a PivotTable to specify the data you want to display. The fields of the source data appear in the PivotTable Field List pane, shown in Exhibit 10-3.

To add fields, you drag a field from the top of the PivotTable Field List pane to one of the four areas at the bottom of the pane, as shown in Exhibit 10-3. You can add more than one field to an area, and you don't need to add all fields to the table. To display data and not just headings, you need to place at least one field in the Σ Values area.

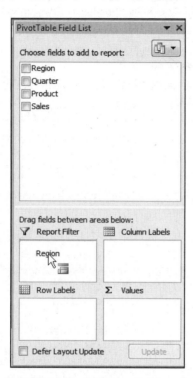

Exhibit 10-3: Adding a field to the PivotTable

Using fields to filter data

After the fields are in place, you can filter the information that appears in the table by selecting options from the Filter columns, Filter rows, or Report Filter lists. For example, you can show all data values or restrict the PivotTable to summarizing only a couple of values.

Following are different ways to filter the PivotTable data shown in Exhibit 10-4:

- To filter data based on the Region field, click the arrow in cell B1. From the list, select the desired region. Check the Select Multiple Items box if you want to select more than one region.

- To filter data based on the Product field, click the arrow in cell B3. From the list, select the desired product.

- To filter data based on the Quarter field, click the arrow in cell A4. From the list, select the desired quarter.

When a filter has been applied, the arrow changes to a filter icon (it looks like a funnel). You can click this icon to display the filter list and see which filter has been applied.

To remove a filter, display the filter list and choose the Clear Filter option. You can also display the filter list by clicking the corresponding filter icon in the PivotTable Field List pane.

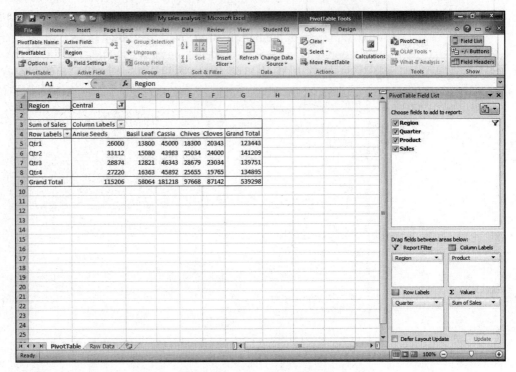

Exhibit 10-4: The PivotTable after fields have been added

Do it!

A-2: Adding fields to a PivotTable

Here's how	Here's why
1 Verify that the PivotTable sheet is active	You'll add fields in the PivotTable layout.
Observe the PivotTable Field List pane	(The entire pane is shown in Exhibit 10-3.) It displays the column headings of the source data in the PivotTable worksheet.
2 Point to **Region**	The pointer turns into a four-headed arrow. You'll use Region as a report filter.
Drag **Region** to the Report Filter box, as shown	In the PivotTable Field List pane.
3 Observe the worksheet	In the worksheet, Region appears with a drop-down arrow in cell A1.
4 In the pane, drag **Quarter** to the Row Labels box	To add Quarter as a row field in the PivotTable.
5 Drag **Product** to the Column Labels box	To add Product as a column field.
6 Drag **Sales** to the Σ Values box	To add Sales as the Values item. The PivotTable shows the sum of the quarterly sales for several products. You can change the view by changing the selections in the Filter Column, Filter Rows, and Region lists.

7 In the worksheet, click as shown

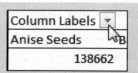

To display a drop-down menu that includes a Product list.

Clear **Basil Leaf**, **Cassia**, and **Cloves**

To specify that the only products shown will be Anise Seeds and Chives.

Click **OK**

Column Labels		
Anise Seeds	Chives	Grand Total
138662	150837	289499
149449	166792	316241
144931	169073	314004
147804	168926	316730
580846	655628	1236474

The worksheet now shows the sales figures for only Anise Seeds and Chives. At the right end of Column Labels, the funnel icon indicates that a filter has been applied.

8 Click as shown

⊿	A	B	
1	Region	(All)	
2			

To display the Region list.

From the Region list, select **Central**

To specify that the view will include the sales of Anise Seeds and Chives in the Central region only.

Click **OK**

To close the list. The PivotTable displays the sales of Anise Seeds and Chives in the Central region.

9 From the Filter Column menu, choose **Clear Filter from "Product"**

To display data for all five products.

10 Update the workbook

Inserting slicers

Explanation

As shown in Exhibit 10-5, the filter icon in cell B1 indicates that the PivotTable is displaying the sales figures for only the Central region. However, when you apply more than one filter, the filter is often labeled as "Multiple items." This designation is not particularly helpful. In Excel 2010, you can insert a slicer to easily show the current filtered state of the data. You can create a slicer for each field in the PivotTable.

Slicers are visual controls you can use to quickly filter your data by selecting values from a list. Slicers are both "live"—they reflect data changes in the underlying PivotTable—and interactive—you can select filter fields on the fly. Slicers appear as separate objects on the worksheet and can be moved around and resized.

To insert a slicer:

1 Select any cell in the PivotTable.

2 Click the PivotTable Tools | Options tab. In the Sort & Filter group, click Insert Slicer. The Insert Slicers dialog box appears with a list of the PivotTable fields.

3 Check the fields you want to display as slicers.

4 Click OK. The slicers appear on top of the PivotTable, and the Slicer Tools | Options tab appears on the Ribbon.

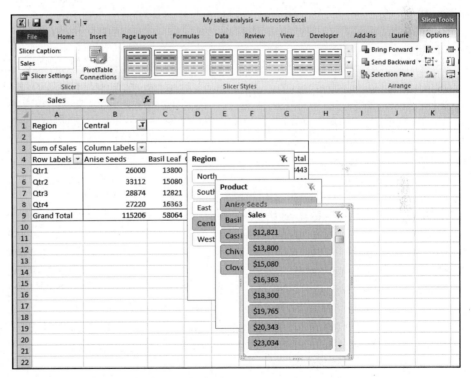

Exhibit 10-5: The PivotTable with slicers

Using slicers to filter data

Even though the slicers are overlapping, it's possible to see which filters are selected, as shown in Exhibit 10-5. The selected items on the slicer indicate which filter is being applied. On the Region slicer, Central is the only highlighted item. The Product slicer indicates that no filter is applied because all items are selected (or highlighted).

To change a slicer filter, click the item you want to use as the filter. Use the Ctrl+click method to select multiple items. Use the Shift+click method to select contiguous items. To clear the filter, click the Clear Filter button at the right end of the slicer header.

Modifying slicers

Excel considers slicers to be shapes. Therefore, you can move, resize, align, and format slicers just as you would other shapes. To move a slicer, drag the slicer header to the desired location. Drag a slicer's border to change the size of the slicer. Use the Slicer Tools | Options tab to apply a slicer style and to align the slicers.

Deleting slicers

You can quickly delete a slicer by selecting it and pressing Delete. You can also right-click the slicer and choose Remove "*Slicer Name*" from the shortcut menu. The slicer is immediately removed.

Do it!

A-3: Using slicers to filter PivotTable data

Here's how	Here's why
1 On the PivotTable Tools | Options tab, in the Sort & Filter group, click **Insert Slicer**	
	The Insert Slicers dialog box opens.
2 Check **Region**, **Product**, and **Sales**	
	To create slicers for the Region, Product, and Sales fields.
3 Click **OK**	As shown in Exhibit 10-5, the three slicers appear overlapped. However, you can see that Central is the only item selected in the Region slicer.
4 Using the slicer headers, drag the slicers so they do not overlap	You can move slicers anywhere on the worksheet. They can even be moved or copied to a separate worksheet. Notice that the Slicer Tools | Options tab has appeared on the Ribbon.
5 On the Region slice, click **North**	
	To change the selected items and display only the North region data.
Press ⌃CTRL and click **South**	To add South to the Region filter. "Multiple items" is displayed next to the Region field label in the worksheet. The slicer provides an easier way to see the applied filters for that field.
6 On the Product slicer, click **Cassia**	To display only the Cassia product sales figures.
Press ⇧SHIFT and click **Cloves**	
	To select Cassia, Chives, and Cloves.

7 On the Slicer Tools | Options tab, click **Selection Pane**

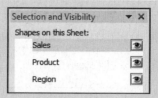

To display the Selection and Visibility pane. The eye icons indicate which slicers are visible. You can click the icon to show or hide the respective slicer.

8 Click **Hide All**

(Located near the bottom of the pane.) To hide all slicers.

Click **Show All**

To show all slicers again. The PivotTable Fields List pane might also appear.

9 For the Product slicer, click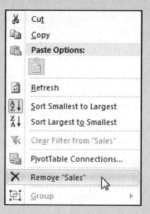

The slicer remains listed in the Selection and Visibility pane, but the empty box indicates that the slicer is hidden.

10 Observe the Sales slicer

When slicers contain a lengthy list of items, you can use the scrollbar to view the additional items.

Right-click the slicer header and choose **Remove "Sales"**

To delete the slicer from the worksheet. It no longer appears in the Selection and Visibility pane.

11 Update and close the workbook

Topic B: Rearranging PivotTables

This topic covers the following Microsoft Office Specialist objectives for exam 77-888: Excel Expert 2010.

#	Objective
3.3	**Apply and manipulate PivotTables**
	3.3.1 Manipulate PivotTable data

Moving fields

Explanation

After creating a PivotTable, you might want to display an entirely different view of the data. You can change the data view by dragging the fields to other areas in the PivotTable. The PivotTable provides options to show or hide the details. To change data in the PivotTable, however, you need to refresh the table after changing the source data.

You can move a field in a PivotTable by dragging the field to a new area in the PivotTable Field List pane. To show a columnar view of the data, as shown in Exhibit 10-6, drag a report or row field to the Column Labels box in the pane. When you want to arrange data in row fields, drag a report or column field to the Row Labels box in the pane.

Sum of Sales	Column Labels ▼				
Row Labels ▼	Qtr1	Qtr2	Qtr3	Qtr4	Grand Total
⊟ Anise Seeds		138662	149449	144931	147804	580846
North		29269	29919	28433	27363	114984
South		12776	12600	12900	13400	51676
East		25617	27818	28224	31321	112980
Central		26000	33112	28874	27220	115206
West		45000	46000	46500	48500	186000
⊟ Basil Leaf	80115	82151	84346	84320	330932
North	16955	15532	17834	16710	67031
South	15435	17345	18200	16982	67962
East	18213	17849	18291	15345	69698
Central	13800	15080	12821	16363	58064
West	15712	16345	17200	18920	68177
⊟ Cassia	238684	240398	250219	247687	976988
North	45643	46989	47897	46876	187405
South	50764	52089	53921	54824	211598
East	44353	43245	42834	41853	172285
Central	45000	43983	46343	45892	181218
West	52924	54092	59224	58242	224482
⊟ Chives	150837	166792	169073	168926	655628
North	37643	38459	37832	35934	149868
South	36935	38922	38395	40242	154494
East	33645	36454	34745	36564	141408

Exhibit 10-6: A PivotTable

Do it!

B-1: Moving fields

The files for this activity are in Student Data folder **Unit 10\Topic B**.

Here's how	Here's why
1 Open Quarters	
Save it as **My quarters**	In the current topic folder.
Observe the PivotTable	It shows the quarterly sales of several products. You'll move the fields to show the data in a different way.
2 In the PivotTable Field List pane, drag **Product** below Quarter, as shown	

The list of products appears beneath each quarter name in the PivotTable.

| 3 Drag **Quarter** to Column Labels | Each quarter appears in a column in the PivotTable. |
| 4 Drag **Region** above Product, as shown | |

To change Region from a report filter to a row label.

Observe the PivotTable	The list of products appears indented beneath each region name in the PivotTable.
5 Drag **Region** below Product	The order of the fields in the Row Labels list affects the structure of the PivotTable.
6 Observe the PivotTable again	The regions and products switch hierarchical order in the spreadsheet, with regions now appearing indented beneath products, as shown in Exhibit 10-6.
7 Update the workbook	

Collapsing and expanding details

Explanation

You can collapse and expand details in a PivotTable that has more than one row or column field. This can help you summarize the data more concisely.

To hide details:

1 Select the cell or range you want to collapse.

2 Click the PivotTable Tools | Options tab.

3 In the Active Field group, click Collapse Entire Field.

To expand a collapsed range, select it and click Expand Entire Field in the Active Field group on the PivotTable Tools | Options tab.

Do it!

B-2: Collapsing and expanding fields

Here's how	Here's why
1 In the PivotTable Field List pane, under Row Labels, drag **Region** above Product	
2 Click the **Options** tab	(If necessary.) Under PivotTable Tools.
Select A5	

Active Field:

Region

Field Settings

Active Field

In the Active Field group, Region appears as the active field.

3 Click	(The Collapse Entire Field button.) To hide the sales details for products and show only the total sales for each region.
Deselect the range	

Sum of Sales	Column Labels				
Row Labels	Qtr1	Qtr2	Qtr3	Qtr4	Grand Total
⊞ North	168402	171468	169938	162776	672584
⊞ South	156152	161980	165738	166260	650130
⊞ East	149506	151044	154530	160748	615828
⊞ Central	123443	141209	139751	134895	539298
⊞ West	183842	191342	200168	201285	776637
Grand Total	781345	817043	830125	825964	3254477

The worksheet shows only the quarterly sales details for each region.

4 Click as shown	

⊞ North
⊞ South
⊞ East

To show the product details for the North region. Next, you'll show all of the details for all regions.

5 Click	(The Expand Entire Field button.) To expand the entire field and show the product sales details for all regions.
6 Update the workbook	

Refreshing PivotTable data

Explanation

You cannot directly change the data in a PivotTable because it's based on source data. To change data in a PivotTable, you must first change the source data and then refresh the PivotTable to reflect the latest changes.

You can refresh the PivotTable by clicking the Refresh button in the Data group on the Options tab.

Do it!

B-3: Refreshing the data in a PivotTable

Here's how	Here's why
1 Select B6	It displays 29269, which is the value of the Qtr 1 sales of Anise Seeds for the North region.
Enter **30000**	When you try to enter the first character, a message box appears with a warning that you can't change the value in a PivotTable.
Click **OK**	To close the message box.
2 Click the Raw Data sheet	This sheet contains the source data for the PivotTable. To change the data in the PivotTable, you have to change the values in the worksheet.
3 Select D46	This cell contains the raw data that appears in cell B6 in the PivotTable. You'll change this value and then view the result in the PivotTable.
Edit D46 to read **30000**	This cell is the only contributor to the value of B6 in the PivotTable.
4 Click the PivotTable sheet	Notice that B6 still shows the old value.
5 Click the **Options** tab	Under PivotTable Tools.
6 In the Data group, click	(The top half of the Refresh button.) To update the PivotTable with the latest data. B6 now shows the new value.
7 Update and close the workbook	

Microsoft Excel

Cannot change this part of a PivotTable report.

OK

Was this information helpful?

Topic C: Formatting PivotTables

Explanation
You can change the format of a PivotTable by using styles and the Field Settings dialog box. You can use styles to format an entire PivotTable in one step. You can use the Field Settings dialog box to change number formats, specify how data is summarized, and show or hide data.

Using styles

To display formatting options that affect the entire PivotTable, click the PivotTable Tools | Design tab. Some of the styles are specifically designed for PivotTables. Exhibit 10-7 shows a sample PivotTable style.

Row Labels	Qtr1	Qtr2	Qtr3	Qtr4	Grand Total
□ North	169133	171468	169938	162776	673315
Anise Seeds	30000	29919	28433	27363	115715
Basil Leaf	16955	15532	17834	16710	67031
Cassia	45643	46989	47897	46876	187405
Chives	37643	38459	37832	35934	149868
Cloves	38892	40569	37942	35893	153296
□ South	156152	161980	165738	166260	650130
Anise Seeds	12776	12600	12900	13400	51676
Basil Leaf	15435	17345	18200	16982	67962
Cassia	50764	52089	53921	54824	211598
Chives	36935	38922	38395	40242	154494
Cloves	40242	41024	42322	40812	164400
□ East	149506	151044	154530	160748	615828
Anise Seeds	25617	27818	28224	31321	112980
Basil Leaf	18213	17849	18291	15345	69698
Cassia	44353	43245	42834	41853	172285
Chives	33645	36454	34745	36564	141408
Cloves	27678	25678	30436	35665	119457
□ Central	123443	141209	139751	134895	539298
Anise Seeds	26000	33112	28874	27220	115206
Basil Leaf	13800	15080	12821	16363	58064
Cassia	45000	43983	46343	45892	181218
Chives	18300	25034	28679	25655	97668
Cloves	20343	24000	23034	19765	87142

Exhibit 10-7: A sample PivotTable style

Do it!

C-1: Applying a PivotTable style

The files for this activity are in Student Data folder **Unit 10\Topic C**.

Here's how	Here's why
1 Open Products	
Save the workbook as **My products**	In the current topic folder.
2 Click the **Design** tab	Under PivotTable Tools.
3 In the PivotTable Styles group, click the More arrow, as shown	 To open the PivotTable Styles gallery.
4 Under Medium, click as shown	 To apply Pivot Style Medium 2 to the PivotTable. The PivotTable appears as shown in Exhibit 10-7.
5 Update the workbook	

Changing field settings

You can change field settings to alter how data appears or is summarized in a PivotTable. To change field settings:

1 Select any cell in the data area.

2 Click the PivotTable Tools | Options tab.

3 In the Active Field group, click Field Settings to open the Value Field Settings dialog box, shown in Exhibit 10-8.

4 Click the Number Format button to open the Format Cells dialog box. Select the desired options and click OK.

5 Click OK.

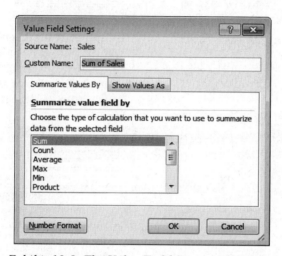

Exhibit 10-8: The Value Field Settings dialog box

Do it!

C-2: Changing field settings

Here's how	Here's why
1 Select B18	(If necessary.) This cell is in the data area. You'll apply a number format to the data items.
2 Click the **Options** tab	Under PivotTable Tools.
3 In the Active Field group, click **Field Settings**	To open the Value Field Settings dialog box, shown in Exhibit 10-8.
4 Click **Number Format**	To open the Format Cells dialog box, with the Number tab active.
From the Category list, select **Currency**	To display the formatting options under Currency. The $ option is selected in the Symbol list. You'll add this prefix symbol to the sales values.
Edit the Decimal places box to read **0**	To specify that currency values should be displayed as whole-dollar amounts.
Click **OK**	To close the Format Cells dialog box.
5 Click **OK**	To close the Value Field Settings dialog box and apply the formatting to all Sales field values (not just the selected cell). The values are now formatted with commas and the $ symbol.
6 Update and close the workbook	

Topic D: Using PivotCharts

This topic covers the following Microsoft Office Specialist objectives for exam 77-888: Excel Expert 2010.

#	Objective
3.4	**Apply and manipulate PivotCharts**
	3.4.1 Create a PivotChart
	3.4.2 Manipulate PivotChart data
	3.4.3 Analyze PivotChart data

Creating PivotCharts

Explanation

You can use a PivotChart to graphically display data from a PivotTable. A single PivotChart provides different views of the same data.

When you create a PivotChart, the row fields of the PivotTable become the categories, and the column fields become the series.

To create a PivotChart, select any cell in a PivotTable and click PivotChart in the Tools group on the PivotTable Tools | Options tab. In the Insert Chart dialog box, select options as you would for a standard chart, and click OK.

You can also create a new PivotChart and PivotTable at the same time. To do so, you select a cell in the source data, click the Insert tab, click the PivotTable button's arrow (in the Tables group), and choose PivotChart.

Changing the view of a PivotChart

In Excel 2010, Microsoft improved the way you change the view of a PivotChart. As shown in Exhibit 10-9, PivotCharts contain field buttons that are used to change what is displayed for a specific field. For example, to change the regions shown in the sample PivotChart, click the Region field button and select the regions you want to show. The same method can be used to filter the Product and Quarter fields.

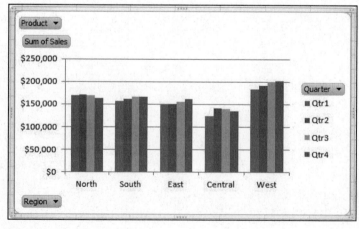

Exhibit 10-9: A PivotChart

Do it!

D-1: Creating a PivotChart

The files for this activity are in Student Data folder **Unit 10\Topic D**.

Here's how	Here's why
1 Open Sales chart	
Save the workbook as **My sales chart**	In the current topic folder.
Click anywhere within the PivotTable	(If necessary.) To indicate which data to use for the PivotChart.
2 Click the **Options** tab	Under PivotTable Tools.
In the Tools group, click **PivotChart**	PivotChart To open the Insert Chart dialog box. You'll create the default Column chart.
Click **OK**	To create a PivotChart in a floating box on this sheet. In the PivotTable Field List pane, the field box titles reflect the Legend and Axis, and the boxes contain the active fields. The chart's X-axis displays the Row Labels fields; the legend displays the Column Labels fields; and the bars represent the data values. You'll change the PivotTable and chart to show only the total sales for each region.
3 In the PivotTable Field List pane, drag **Product** to Report Filter	 To make Product the report filter. You can now sort and filter data by product in the PivotChart.
Observe the PivotChart	As shown in Exhibit 10-9, the total sales for the five regions appear in columns, and each column is divided into quarters. You can use the Product, Region, and Quarter buttons to change the data displayed in the PivotChart.
Resize and move the chart so it does not overlap the table	Drag the chart box's edges and corners as necessary.

4 On the PivotChart, click **Product**, as indicated

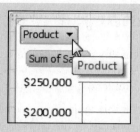

To display the Product items.

Select **Basil Leaf**

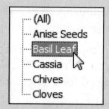

To show only the Basil Leaf data in the PivotChart.

Click **OK**

The PivotChart displays the total sales of only Basil Leaf for all regions. The axis scale has adjusted to reflect the filtered figures.

5 From the Quarter list, clear all of the options except Qtr1

Click **OK**

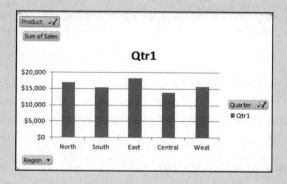

The chart displays the total sales of Basil Leaf in the first quarter for all regions. The Product and Quarter buttons contain icons indicating that the chart data has been filtered.

6 Update and close the workbook

Unit summary: PivotTables and PivotCharts

Topic A   In this topic, you learned that a **PivotTable** is used to summarize, organize, and compare large amounts of data in a worksheet. You created a PivotTable and added **fields** to the layout of a PivotTable. You also inserted **slicers** to filter the data.

Topic B   In this topic, you changed the view of data in a PivotTable by moving the **row** and **column fields** to different areas. You also learned how to **hide** and **show details** in the PivotTable.

Topic C   In this topic, you applied **styles** to format a PivotTable. You also used the Value Field Settings dialog box to apply formatting to numerical data.

Topic D   In this topic, you learned that a **PivotChart** graphically displays data from a PivotTable, and you created a PivotChart. You also used the **field buttons** to change which data is displayed for a specific field in a PivotChart.

Independent practice activity

In this activity, you'll create a PivotTable, modify it, and apply a style to it. Then you'll create and modify a PivotChart.

The files for this activity are in Student Data folder **Unit 10\Unit summary**.

1 Open Sales 2005-2009.

2 Save the workbook as **My sales 2005-2009**.

3 Create a PivotTable based on the data in the Raw Data worksheet. (*Hint:* Select any cell in the data, and click the PivotTable button on the Insert tab.)

4 Move Year to the Row Labels area, move Quarter to the Column Labels area, move Product to the Row Labels area (below the Year field), and move Sales to the Σ Values area.

5 Apply the Pivot Style Medium 3 style to the PivotTable. Compare your results with Exhibit 10-10.

6 Create a basic column PivotChart. (*Hint:* Use the PivotTable Tools | Options tab.)

7 Make **Quarter** and **Year** report filters in the PivotChart. (*Hint:* Drag the fields to Report Filters.)

8 Change the PivotChart to display the sales in the fourth quarter of 2009.

9 Compare your results with Exhibit 10-11.

10 Update and close the workbook.

11 Close Excel.

Sum of Sales	Column Labels ▼				
Row Labels ▼	Qtr1	Qtr2	Qtr3	Qtr4	Grand Total
⊟ 2005	123443	141209	139751	134895	539298
Anise Seeds	26000	33112	28874	27220	115206
Basil Leaf	13800	15080	12821	16363	58064
Cassia	45000	43983	46343	45892	181218
Chives	18300	25034	28679	25655	97668
Cloves	20343	24000	23034	19765	87142
⊟ 2006	139490.59	159566.17	157918.63	152431.35	609406.74
Anise Seeds	29380	37416.56	32627.62	30758.6	130182.78
Basil Leaf	15594	17040.4	14487.73	18490.19	65612.32
Cassia	50850	49700.79	52367.59	51857.96	204776.34
Chives	20679	28288.42	32407.27	28990.15	110364.84
Cloves	22987.59	27120	26028.42	22334.45	98470.46
⊟ 2007	165413.62	189220.06	187266.34	180759.3	722659.32
Anise Seeds	34840	44370.08	38691.16	36474.8	154376.04
Basil Leaf	18492	20207.2	17180.14	21926.42	77805.76
Cassia	60300	58937.22	62099.62	61495.28	242832.12
Chives	24522	33545.56	38429.86	34377.7	130875.12
Cloves	27259.62	32160	30865.56	26485.1	116770.28
⊟ 2008	194706.6439	222728.9557	220429.2523	212769.8835	850634.7354
Anise Seeds	41009.8	52227.5576	45542.9602	42934.106	181714.4238
Basil Leaf	21766.74	23785.684	20222.5633	25809.3599	91584.3472
Cassia	70978.5	69374.3859	73096.8139	72385.4516	285835.1514
Chives	28864.59	39486.1282	45235.3867	40465.6315	154051.7364

▶ ▶| **Sheet1** / Raw Data /

Exhibit 10-10: The PivotTable after Step 5

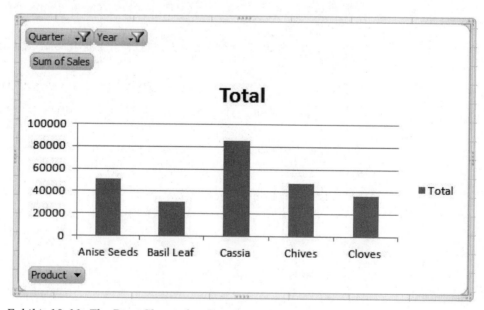

Exhibit 10-11: The PivotChart after Step 8

Review questions

1 What is a PivotTable?

2 How do you start creating a PivotTable?

3 Can you directly change the data in a PivotTable? If not, how do you change the data?

4 Which PivotTable feature is used to easily identify the current filters applied to the data?

   A Row labels

   B PivotChart

   C Slicers

   D Field list

5 Why would you use a PivotChart?

6 How do you create a PivotChart?

Course summary

This summary contains information to help you bring the course to a successful conclusion. Using this information, you will be able to:

A Use the summary text to reinforce what you've learned in class.

B Determine the next courses in this series (if any), as well as any other resources that might help you continue to learn about Excel 2010.

Topic A: Course summary

Use the following summary text to reinforce what you've learned in class.

Unit summaries

Unit 1

In this unit, you switched between workbooks and copied a worksheet to another workbook. You created **3-D formulas** to perform calculations based on data from multiple worksheets, and you added a **Watch window**. Then, you created and modified **links** to data in a different workbook, and saw that Excel automatically updates data in the destination workbook when the data is changed in the source workbook. Finally, you saved an arrangement of open workbooks as a **workspace**.

Unit 2

In this unit, you applied **special number formats** to ZIP codes and phone numbers, and you controlled the display of zero values. Then, you created **custom number formats**. Next, you used formulas to format text. You observed Excel's built-in **styles** and **themes**, and learned how to create, modify, and apply styles and themes. You **merged cells**, changed the orientation of text in cells, split merged cells, and used **Paste Special** operations. Finally, you added color and a watermark to a worksheet background.

Unit 3

In this unit, you created an **outline** to summarize data by levels, and used the **Consolidate** command to summarize data from several ranges. Next, you created **custom views** to save different sets of worksheet display and print settings. Finally, you created automatic **subtotals** to divide a list with summary information.

Unit 4

In this unit, you created and edited **named ranges** to make formulas easier to understand. You used these names in formulas, and created names automatically from row and column headings. Finally, you created **3-D names** that span multiple sheets.

Unit 5

In this unit, you learned about the structure of worksheet data, and you **sorted** data by the information in one or more of its columns. You also used the **AutoFilter** command to display only rows that meet certain criteria. Next, you used the **Custom AutoFilter** dialog box to specify multiple conditions, using comparison criteria and comparison operators. Then, you created a **criteria range** to specify complex search conditions based on multiple column headings, and you **copied filtered data** to a new location. You then created and renamed **tables**, added rows and columns, and used **structured references** in table-related formulas.

Unit 6

In this unit, you saved a worksheet as a **Web page** and used the Web Page Preview command. Then, you published a worksheet as a Web page and used the AutoRepublish feature. Next, you inserted, modified, and deleted **hyperlinks** in a workbook. You learned that clicking a hyperlink opens a Web page in a browser. Finally, you learned how to share workbook files by sending them as **e-mail attachments**.

Unit 7

In this unit, you adjusted the scale of a **chart**. You formatted **data points** and exploded slices in a pie chart to highlight data. Then, you created a combination chart by using two value axes. You also added a **trendline** to a chart and inserted **sparklines** in a worksheet. You also used **chart templates**. Then, you added, formatted, and moved **drawing objects** and shapes in a chart. Finally, you inserted a picture in a worksheet.

Unit 8

In this unit, you used the Formula Auditing tools to **trace** precedent and dependent cells and to trace errors. Next, you added **comments** to worksheets and workbooks. Then, you **protected** a worksheet to prevent unauthorized users from making changes, and you unlocked cells that users should be allowed to modify. You also protected the **workbook structure** from changes. Next, you learned about digital signatures. Then, you **shared workbooks** and merged copies of shared workbooks. You **tracked changes** in a workbook and accepted or rejected tracked changes. Finally, you used the **Document Inspector** and marked a workbook as final.

Unit 9

In this unit, you learned about Excel's **application settings**, and you changed settings that control the way Excel operates and displays data. Next, you used **templates** to create documents such as sales invoices. Then, you created and modified templates. Finally, you learned how to specify an alternate location for template files.

Unit 10

In this unit, you created a **PivotTable**. You added fields, changed views, and created **slicers** for the PivotTable. Then, you formatted PivotTable data by applying a style and changing field settings. Finally, you created **PivotCharts** to graphically display the PivotTable data.

Topic B: Continued learning after class

It is impossible to learn how to use any software effectively in a single day. To get the most out of this class, you should begin working with Excel 2010 to perform real tasks as soon as possible. We also offer resources for continued learning.

Next courses in this series

- *Excel 2010: Advanced*
  - Use the IF, OR, IFERROR, SUMIF, nested IF, and ROUND functions
  - Use PMT, date and time functions, and array formulas
  - Use lookup functions and create data tables
  - Use the Data Validation feature and database functions
  - Export Excel data and import XML data from external databases
  - Use the Goal Seek and Solver utilities
  - Record, edit, and run macros

Other resources

For more information, visit www.axzopress.com.

Glossary

3-D formula
A formula that refers to the same cell or range in multiple worksheets.

Cell orientation
The direction of text flow in a cell.

Combination chart
A single chart that includes two or more graph types.

Conditional formatting
Formatting that is applied to data only if a specific criterion is met.

Criteria range
A group of cells that contain a set of search conditions.

Dependent cell
A cell that relies on the value of another cell.

Destination workbook
A workbook that contains a formula with an external reference.

Digital certificate
An attachment that guarantees security for a file.

Digital signature
An electronic security stamp that is used to authenticate files that are sent over the Internet.

External reference
The part of a formula in one workbook that refers to a cell, range, or name in another workbook. Also called an "external link."

Field
A column of data in a database. Also, a category of data in a PivotTable.

Field name
A column heading, which appears in the first row of a range or table.

Leader line
A line used in a chart to connect a data label to its associated data point.

Outline
A method of organizing worksheet data by grouping it in various levels of detail.

PivotChart
A chart created from PivotTable data. The row fields of the PivotTable become the categories, and the column fields become the series. Click the field buttons in the PivotChart to change what the chart displays.

PivotTable
An interactive table that summarizes, organizes, and compares large amounts of data in a worksheet. You can rotate the rows and columns in a PivotTable to obtain different views of the same data.

Precedent cell
A cell that provides data to another cell.

Print title
Text that you want to print as a heading on all pages.

Record
A row of data in a range or table.

Sizing handles
Handles that appear as small squares or circles around the border of a selected picture and that are used to change its height and width.

Slicer
A PivotTable feature that is used to filter data.

Sorting
The process of arranging data in ascending or descending order according to the contents of one or more columns in the range.

Source data
The data on which a PivotTable is based.

Source workbook
The workbook to which an external reference refers.

Sparkline
A small chart that is inserted into a single cell to illustrate a pattern or trend in data.

Structured reference
A reference that uses a table name or column heading (or both), instead of a cell or range address, in a formula that refers to table data.

Style
A collection of formats that are saved and applied as a group.

Table

A series of rows containing related data; you must define the range as a table in order to use certain table-related features in Excel.

Template

A workbook with predefined settings on which you can base new workbooks.

Trendline

A graphical representation of drifts or variations in a data series.

Watch window

A dialog box that displays values and formulas in a linked worksheet without your having to navigate there.

Workspace

A logical container of related workbooks that retains page setups, window sizes, and display settings.

Index

U